Women Write Resistance: Poets Resist Gender Violence
Copyright © 2013 Laura Madeline Wiseman

Hyacinth Girl Press is a micro-press that specializes in handmade books of smaller press runs. The ultimate goal of Hyacinth Girl Press is to bring feminism, mysticism, and scientific inquiry together with awesome poetry. For more information, please visit www.HyacinthGirlPress.com

Editor: Margaret Bashaar

Layout and Design: Adam Wagler

Cover Art: Elayne Safir
emptyminute.com

Library of Congress Cataloguing in Publication Data
Laura Madeline Wiseman; Women Write Resistance
ISBN Number 978-0-615-77278-3

WOMEN WRITE RESISTANCE

poets resist gender violence

Edited by Laura Madeline Wiseman

H G P

Hyacinth Girl Press

www.hyacinthgirlpress.com

TABLE OF CONTENTS

PREFACE

The seed for this anthology, *Women Write Resistance: Poets Resist Gender Violence* started in a coffee shop, mid-afternoon, mid-week, in the middle of a Midwest City. I had recently started a Ph.D. program in English and was taking three classes—the pedagogy class required for all teaching assistants, a course in Chicana literature and theory, and a graduate poetry workshop. Inspired by the feminist theory I'd studied in my M.A. program in women's studies and the reading I was doing in the literature class, I began writing poems about the Juarez murders—the hundreds of women murdered in Juarez, Mexico. I'd been thinking about gender violence for a long time. I'd volunteered and worked in domestic violence shelters, marched in Take Back the Night, and taught poetry workshops at women's crisis centers, while also reading deeply in research and theory on trauma, PTSD, and violence against women. I'd always disagreed with W. H. Auden's statement that "poetry makes nothing happen." To me, poetry was action, poetry did make things happen, or at the very least, had the potential to initiate action. As I sat in the coffee shop, amid the cool blasts of air from the front door, the hiss and gurgle of the espresso machine, and the hum of conversation, I wondered about my work as a poet, teacher, and scholar. Was there anything I could do about gender violence?

I decided to put together this anthology of poems about gender violence written by over one hundred American women poets with a critical introduction framing poetry as action. Over the next five years and while I was working on my Ph.D., I read hundreds of journals, poetry collections, and anthologies searching for these poems and researched theory on gender violence. For a class in American poetry, I proposed to write the critical introduction for this anthology as the term project. For my comprehensive exams and reading lists, I selected poetry that explored gender violence such as work by Audre Lorde, Sharon Olds, Joy Harjo, and Lucille Clifton and wrote a critical essay on the way poems by Judy Grahn, Minnie Bruce Pratt, and Chrystos could be tools for activism. I wrote more papers and presented at conferences—NACCS, AWP, NWSA, Split this Rock— on trauma, gender violence, and poetry. Meanwhile, I also passed the comps, proposed a dissertation topic, wrote the dissertation, defended the dissertation, and graduated. At the beginning of the sixth year in researching this project, I was ready. I found a press—a micro-feminist press. I contacted poets from my researched list who were alive, who were women, and who were American. I held to these original constraints because I wanted contemporary writers. I wanted women writers because women are proportionally the victims of gender violence. I wanted American poets because I wanted the focus to be on gender violence in American and/or American perspectives of gender violence elsewhere. I asked these poets if I could include their poem(s) or to submit new work. I sought permissions. I posted a call for poems to round out the collection. I received hundreds of poems. I read the submissions. Finally, I accepted just over one hundred poets, well aware that there were more poets and poems out there—indeed I found additional poets, but the book was too far along in press.

In some ways, this anthology is two things—a critical essay that frames poetry about gender violence as action and a collection of poems I believe do the work outlined in the essay. I see them working together—the essay is the critical framework for what the poems creatively do. Together, they are a tool to create dialogue about gender violence, poetry, and action. It is the hope that *Women Write Resistance* offers readers various strategies to resist violence against women. This anthology can be used as a classroom text in women's studies classes, sociology classes, and literature classes; as a tool for professionals working with women and children in crisis; as a book adopted for a book club; as a text in contemporary conscious raising groups; as a personal poetry anthology one thumbs through in a coffee shop; or in any number of settings. Poetry is action, a revolution of language. *Women Write Resistance* challenges readers to find their method for social change and act.

Reader, what will you do?

Laura Madeline Wiseman, Ph.D.
February, 2013
Lincoln, Nebraska

CRITICAL INTRODUCTION

> *Revolution is poetry.*
> ~Adrienne Rich[1]

Poetry as power. Poetry as action. Poets have described the potential of poetry to foster change in the lives of one and of many. From Adrienne Rich to Pablo Neruda, Percy Byron Shelly to Ralph Waldo Emerson, Audre Lorde to Czeslaw Misosz, all of these poets wr ite of poetry's power for action. Muriel Rukeyser writes "If there were no poetry on any day in the world, poetry would be invented that day" (*Lofty Dogmas*, 355). Milosz writes, "Do not feel safe. The poet remembers. You can kill one, but another is born" (406-407). Adrienne Rich explains one must write the "words you have dreaded and needed in order to know you exist" (33-34). *Women Write Resistance: Poets Resist Gendered Violence* collects poetry of resistance written by over one hundred American women poets. They break silences about violence against women as they raise consciousness and enact a poetry of witness that links the personal, political, and social. They disrupt hegemonic narratives on gendered violence by employing sassing language and strategic anger. They resist gender violence by earmarking poetry as action. What follows is an account of the overarching theoretical standpoints and framework from which this anthology emerges.

> *Death only uses violence/ when there is any kind of resistance.*
> ~Judy Grahn, "A Woman is Talking to Death" (117)

Resistance

Gender violence is pervasive and multi-dimensional, the effects of which may last a lifetime, may carry over into future generations, and may perpetuate a culture in which violence is the norm or normalized and thus made invisible. *Women Write Resistance* uses the terms "violence against women" and "gender violence" and defines them *as any act or omission that results in serious injury to a woman, child, or another based on gender.*[2] This definition privileges the words *gender* and *women* to signal the significance gender plays within incidents of violence, to highlight how violence is disproportionately perpetrated by men to women, and to remind us that sexism, patriarchy, and misogyny continue to mark certain acts of violence against women permissible. Finally, this anthology defines these terms to highlight whose voices readers will find within *Women Write Resistance:* the voices of women.

Within the rhetoric of empowering those who have experienced violence, often the term "victim" is used to describe those who are currently abused by an abuser. Once someone escapes the violent situation and thus, survives the abuse, one is denoted as the survivor. In her study of sexual violence, Tami Spry conjectures that patriarchal narrations of violence focus and confine subjects' understanding of self only in relation to the violent act(s). Such linguistic positioning posits the individual as the passive recipient and always in relation to the one who perpetrated the abuse; she is the victim or she is the survivor. Spry writes, "Survivor/victim categories perpetuate and reify the powerful symbol of the powerless woman" (27). Once one is victimized s/he is always marked by that violence. The narrative of the "powerless woman" became the only visible narrative because other aspects were erased by dominate discourses.

Though "survivor" offers women a path to empowerment, the victim/survivor terminology fails to offer up new ways of conceptualizing other relationships or stances one might assume in regards to violence; such narratives do little to effectively delineate the actual and diverse experiences of individual women who experience gender violence. Spry suggests the victim/survivor dichotomy negates the possibility for women to obtain agency because their positionality is always bound to the phallus. She writes, "[s]he is already and always held in relation to the phallus; she is victim to it or survivor of it" (27). This anthology would like to advocate for and take up a third category to disrupt this dichotomy and employ this concept to describe poetic strategies to challenge violence. This category is a "resister." A resister is one who resists for herself, her community, and society at large. A resister may have experienced violence personally or she may not have, but the position of a resister facilitates and advocates for agency. These poets are actors, rather than reactionaries. These poets resist by arming themselves with poems.

In her landmark article, "Mapping the Margins: Intersectionality, Identity Politics, and Violence Against Women of Color," Kimberlé Williams Crenshaw articulates a necessary and vital reconfiguration of discussions on gender violence with close attention to race and other marginalized identities. Crenshaw argues that "ignoring differences *within* groups frequently contributes to tension *among* groups" (94). She points to locales where race intersects with other identities that put women of color at further disadvantages such as structural intersectionalities like poverty, unemployment, language barriers, and political intersectionalities of "overlapping systems of subordination," like racism combined with sexism (111). In her introduction to her poem "A Woman is Talking to Death," Judy Grahn interrogates intersections of oppression to call attention to the interconnectedness of personal, political, and social violence. She explains her process writing that poem: "The particular challenges of this poem for me were how to discuss the criss-cross oppressions which people use against each other and which continually divide us—and how to define a lesbian life within the context of other people in the world" (112). Though identities like race, gender, and sexuality are social constructions, this does not mean that those social constructions do not have a materiality that informs the ways people conduct and experience their lives. Crenshaw writes, "Through an awareness of intersectionality, we can better acknowledge and ground the differences among us and negotiate the means by which these differences will find expression in constructing group politics" (115).

> *Words are also actions, and actions are a kind of words.*
> -Ralph Waldo Emerson[3]

> *You must write, and read as if your life depended on it.*
> -Adrienne Rich[4]

Differential Consciousness

The poems in *Women Write Resistance* resist gender violence. The literary mechanisms by which resistance occurs is as diverse and dimensional as gender violence itself. The poets in this anthology engage in a radical, multi-layered, dynamic strategy of resistance that uses various modes of activism which are deployed as needed. To explain what this might look like, I would like to take up the work Chela Sandoval theorizes in *Methodology of the Oppressed*. She challenges notions of oppression and argues that fractured identities are not a new phenomenon experienced only in a postmodern world, but rather the continual and historical experiences of those who are oppressed. She argues that the oppressed resist oppression through what she defines as "differential consciousness."

Sandoval begins with postmodernism and the lamentation by some theorists of fractured identities which may cause schizophrenic renderings of experience. Other feminists, such as Crenshaw noted above, have pointed to multiple and intersecting identities as sites of power, rather than sites of weakness. Biddy Martin and Chandra Talpade Mohanty suggest that one should sustain "complex positionalities" to preclude settling into one identity. Under this framework, creating complex identities are intentional acts by a poet as a mode to resist the tendency of power and a patriarchal culture to maneuver oppressed groups into confining labels and categories. To illustrate an account of a methodology of the oppressed, Sandoval reads the ideological positions women took up to articulate and embody activist stances to confront the patriarchy during the second wave of the feminist movement. She locates four sites of hegemonic feminist work: liberal (women and men are the same), Marxist (women are different from men), radical/cultural (women are superior), and socialist (women are a racially divided class) (9). Sandoval then posits a more encompassing site: differential consciousness. Differential consciousness is the fifth category in this taxonomy and has the ability to move between and among the first four. It is a "*tactical* weaponry for confronting the shifting currents of power" (14). Sandoval uses strategies of feminists to articulate one site of differential consciousness. She suggests that the oppressed have been criticized for lack of loyalty within a given movement. She argues that it is not disloyalty, but rather that the methodology of the oppressed allows for the flexibility to take up and abandon various resistance strategies as needed.

Unlike other theories to understand power which might suggest a top-down or hierarchical model, Sandoval's model suggests that power is not something that oppressors have and various oppressed groups vie for, but rather that power is diffused through a matrix structure where there are nexuses of power, but no central or stable site for it to reside. Differential consciousness as strategy is therefore "a kinetic motion" which allows individuals to move back and forth between and among resistance approaches while not privileging one "over any other" (54.5). Such a plan is necessary within a structure with various nodes of power because it gives practitioners "grace, flexibility, and strength" (60.1). It allows for a "*tactical subjectivity* with the capacity to recenter depending upon the kinds of oppression to be confronted" (14).[5] The ability to organize around one form of resistance by using one tactic to confront and then recenter around another form is vital for resistance to oppressive powers. The oppressed maintain shifting fronts as their strategy of resistance. Sandoval writes, "This process of taking and using whatever is necessary and available in order to negotiate, confront, or speak to power—and then moving on to new forms, expressions, and ethos when necessary…" is the action platform of the oppressed (28.9).

Differential consciousness resists the simplistic notions of losing/winning, failing/succeeding, beginning/ending. In a teleological frame, time is chronological and all events are viewed as cause and effect, as operating within binaries. But linearity limits a complex understanding of movement, resistance, and action. To view activism as "mobile" with a "kinetic motion that maneuvers, poetically transfigures, and orchestrates while demanding alienation, perversion, and reformation in both spectators and practitioners," is to mark resistance as multilayered and not contingent on individual losses and gains (3).[6] It is the shuttling between various resistance modes that is necessary to critique, subvert, and challenge oppressors.

Women Write Resistance takes up Sandoval's differential consciousness in two ways. First, I would like to suggest that poetics and specifically, poetry of resistance, acts as differential consciousness by allowing poets to use multiple strategies to challenge the powers that endorse gender violence. Identities and intersections of identities inform how a poet might activate a resistance front and thus, a tool box of resistance tactics is necessary. To critique violence, and specifically gender violence, positions the practitioner outside of the hegemony. As Sandoval writes, indeed to employ such tactics means one is often already an outsider, one who has "a lack of loyalty to dominant ideological signification, combined with intellectual curiosity that demands an explosion of meaning…for the sake either of survival or of political change toward equality" (179). If poetry is action, if poetry is power, and if poetry is revolution, or at the very least has the potential to be, differential consciousness offers multiple paths a poet might take to rupture the cultural meanings of gender violence.

Secondly, I would like to suggest that like the individual poets in this text, the text *Women Write Resistance* as a whole enacts differential consciousness. Sandoval writes on semiotics and the languages of emancipation that differential consciousness is a movement which builds "on old categories of meaning in order to transform" them by "suggesting something else, something beyond them" (84.5). Poetry gives readers and writers an opportunity to transform the culture, their lives, and the language. Sandoval writes that revolutionary language is a "simultaneous destruction and remaking of the world" (107). *Women Write Resistance* seeks to operate on various nodes and locales to intercede on the behalf of all women and resist gender violence. Recognizing the necessity of a variety of practices to resist violence, *Women Write Resistance's* tool is poetry and within poetry there are numerous shifting fronts of resistance. The following outlines the strategies readers will find in this anthology.

> *In a room where people unanimously maintain a conspiracy of silence,*
> *one word of truth sounds like a pistol shot.*
> – Milosz, "Nobel Prize Lecture" (411)

Breaking Silences

Breaking silence is one strategy of differential consciousness poets draw on to resist gender violence. In the United States, a silence has surrounded intellectual, legal, and community discussions on violence. Social norms, cultural values, myths, and stereotypes have pervaded in the past and continue to delineate who can speak about violence, what that reveals about the speaker, and who's voice is valued. The rhetoric of "victim-blaming" stigmatizes those who do speak by creating a culture in which victims are shown to have asked for it. This creates a perception of two types of victims: good victims and bad victims. Good victims are often depicted in unrealistic terms and bad victims are made to seem to deserve the violence inflicted on them. Victim-blaming and silence about gender violence persist. In her essay, "Silence: A Rhetorical Art for Resisting Disciplines(s)," scholar Cheryl Glenn considers the rhetoric of silence and calls the speaking/silence binary for women a "double bind: keep silent or speak and be shamed" (268). When a woman does break silence, she ruptures deep-seated culture secrecies that value the public/private division. Because silence and language work together, to break silence is to make transparent those secrets about violence that oppress women.

Identities overlap, intersect, and inform the stakes of breaking silence and the social risks for speaking out. It is true that all women risk something in breaking silence, but privilege informs the degree of risk one takes. In order to read the silences and speaking of Anita Hill, Glenn argues that "silence is an absence with a function" and "silence and language work together" (263). Glenn suggests that "when Hill was silent, she held power over the men who didn't know what she knew...But as soon as she spoke, the male senators sat silently, judging her" (266). Tami Spry reads this speaking/silence code as one written on the body of women. She argues that when women are victims of sexual violence, their body is taken away from them through acts of violence. She writes, "When the body is erased or used as a symbol to silence itself, knowledge situated within the body is unavailable to the self, or if discovered, ridiculed as base or profane" (27). When Hill experienced the assaults, her body was rendered illegitimate by power and no longer a site of knowledge because her knowledge about her body (if spoken) was a direct challenge to the patriarchal hegemonic discourse that dictates the narratives on sexual violence. By remaining silent she held power. Glenn writes that "when nonwhite overachieving women [later] come out of their silence they can deploy their resistance to greater influence than they might ever have if they had spoken and been heard at the time. And such resistance can be used to confront, resist, and transform" (281). To extend this argument to *Women Write Resistance*, when nonwhite women, lesbians, and other minority poets break silence, they risk more—they risk not being heard, they risk critiquing the communities that support them, they risk ridicule by a hegemonic culture, they risk further modes of oppression that may mark their voices as invalid. But more importantly, when they do break silences, their voices have the potential to echo far and wide. When poets speak to power by breaking silences, they deploy such speech acts as a form of resistance.

Breaking silence risks cultural and identity sanctions, but the mechanisms by which these silences are shattered make such speaking a force with which to be reckoned. Lorde tells us "there are so many silences to be broken" (44). How does one break a silence? From what standpoint does one assume? Poets in *Women Write Resistance* speak of the injustices in their lives and the lives of women they know. Personal experience is one site of authoritative knowledge these poets deploy. They tell us who they are, what they've witnessed, and what it means. Research tells us gendered violence causes deep, emotional and psychological consequences for women, their families, their communities, and society at large. Personal experiences are valuable sources of personal and community awareness. Pablo Neruda explains that poetry's function is to communicate: "All paths lead to the same goal: to convey to others what we are" (105). When poets in *Women Write Resistance* speak, they break silence as witnesses, victims, survivors, and resisters of violence. They speak and present themselves as models for those who cannot speak, those who are not yet ready to speak, or those who did not know that speaking was an option of resistance. Breaking silence is one tool of poetic resistance, but one of many these poets have at their disposal.

Raising Consciousness & Poetry of Witness

The second wave of the feminist movement is often characterized by consciousness raising, a practice linking personal experiences, including trauma and violence, to larger political situations (e.g. oppression) to make meaning of one's life. It is and was characterized by the phrase *the personal is political*. Rukeyser writes, "For poetry is, at every instant, concerned with meaning. The poet—of the kind of poetry for which I hope—knows that consciousness and creation are linked, and cannot be postponed" (*Lofty Dogmas*, 356). Poetry is a meaning-making animal that uses the tools of language to make connections between emotions, the body, place, culture, and society. In the introduction to *Against Forgetting: Twentieth Century Poetry of Witness* (1993) Carolyn Forché explores how she used her poetry to make meaning of her personal experiences in writing her first book *The Country Between Us* (1981), a collection that described her witnessing the atrocities of war. Forché defines her terms within the second feminist wave rhetoric. She writes, "Poetry of witness presents the reader with an interesting interpretive problem.... The distinction between the personal and the political give the political realm too much and too little scope; at the same time, it renders the personal too important and not important enough. If we give up the dimension of the personal, we risk relinquishing one of the most powerful sites of resistance" (31). She argues for a new way to read poetry through a triad of personal-political-social, and thus expands the work of *the personal is political*. It is this three pronged poetic beast we call today, poetry of witness. Forché continues, "...we should not consider our social lives as merely the products of our choice: the social is a place of resistance and struggle, where books are published, poems read, and protest disseminated. It is the sphere in which claims against the political order are made in the name of justice" (31) and "The poetry of witness reclaims the social from the political and in so doing defends the individual against illegitimate forms of coercion. It often seeks to register through indirection and intervention the ways in which the linguistic and moral universes have been disrupted by events" (45).

Many contemporary poetic work could fall into the category of poetry of witness. For example, the first "Split this Rock Poetry Festival: Poetry of Provocation and Witness" in 2008, included featured speakers such as Forché, Alicia Ostriker, Naomi Shihab Nye, Mark Doty, and many others. In *Women Write Resistance,* poets raise consciousness by modeling the connection of the personal, social, and political. Other poets present historical and contemporary accounts of criminal investigations, murders, and violence against women. Such socially accepted locations of truth are difficult to question and hard to deny. For to question one site of knowledge, would risk questioning all. These poets question and ask readers to do the same. These poets urge readers to see how social institutions inform who we are and what we're able to do. Questioning the social and political aspects of a society and what that means on a personal level is yet another poetic front in differential consciousness.

> No explanation except: the one who tells the tale/ gets to name the monster.
> ~Minne Bruce Pratt "Crime Against Nature" (115)

Disrupting Narratives

Poets in *Women Write Resistance* do not accept the cultural narratives on gendered violence. Predominate narratives available in culture about violence against women are hegemonic in nature, meaning they support and celebrate power structures by erasing, mitigating, or silencing other possible accounts. To challenge narratives within culture is no easy task, but one way to do so is through poetry. Trinh T. Minh-ha argues that all writing is marked by gender and the hegemonic institutions that structure society. She writes that a woman "must *learn* to paint her world with colors chosen more often than not by men for men to suit their realities" (27). It is writing she considers as the theoretical and political work needed to create new truths (22). She argues for a blurry "borderline between theoretical and non-theoretical" work, a place where "theory and poetry necessarily mesh" for a space of freedom (42). To disrupt a narrative of the hegemony is to operate from a place of freedom and from a liberatory epistemology. Such practices critique and challenge narratives on gendered violence.

One place hegemonic narratives exist is the media, a media that does not represent the full story. In her analysis, Nancy Berns explains, "Because individuals use the media to make sense of social problems, it is important to understand how these media construct images of an issue" (264). Cultural narratives rarely extend beyond abstract descriptors of gender violence or their graphic equivalents; they also do not discuss the implications of violence against women. The consequences of violence against women are obscured when newspapers, videogames, films, and television programs depict violence in superficial or sexualized ways, when violence is disregarded or glorified, and when victims of violence are dehumanized. There are occasional ruptures to accounts of gender violence available by the hegemony. When the media does permit gendered violence to be told from perspectives that could critique violence, these depictions frequently sensationalize by presenting stories that titillate. This depiction reinforces and supports hegemonic gendered violence narratives by devaluing them to tabloid status and thereby disallowing them to critique or challenge. Such depictions make light of violence and do not offer individuals the complete version of the effects of violence. Poets of resistance challenge such depictions and describe the profound psychological effects of violence and how it shapes their decisions and actions.

Poets in *Women Write Resistance* contest narratives offered in the media and they do so by poetry. Audre Lorde suggests the importance of poetry for women: "For women, then, poetry is not a luxury. It is a vital necessity of our existence. It forms the quality of the light within which we predicate our hopes and dreams toward survival and change, first made into language, then into idea, then into more tangible action. Poetry is the way we help give name to the nameless so it can be thought" (*Poetry*, 370). Poets disrupt, re-write, and challenge conventional narratives on gendered violence by pointing to alternative narratives, narratives arrived at through poetry. These alternative narratives are subversive and dangerous because they critique violence myths which perpetuate stereotypes and promote ignorance, logical fallacies, and fear. The poems in *Women Write Resistance* do more than speak to power. They resist abuses of power to claim power over their experiences and stories missing from culture at large. They challenge power by disrupting it through poetry. As they do so, these poems invite readers to think through the narratives we might otherwise take for granted.

> Give/ me a word for pain that's sharp enough.
> ~Chrystos "Accident" (4)

Sassing Language

It is not just the narratives that poets in *Women Write Resistance* defy. It is the language itself. Poets take up the power to name and talk about the violence *in* and *on* their *own terms*. Readers will find a language of sass not often found in conventional poetry. To some readers unfamiliar with the wide possibility of writing styles within American poetry, certain poetic strategies might appear anti-literary. However, American poetry has a long tradition of using language as the site of resistance by such poets as Walt Whitman, H.D., Langston Hughes, Gertrude Stein, Allen Ginsberg, and many, many others. As Mary K. DeShazer asserts of poems that resist, they "challenge traditional generic and formal categories by breaking down conventional literary divisions and hierarchies…" (10).

To sass, *Women Write Resistance* poets subvert the language. They employ literary tactics to name their experiences within personal terms. Sometimes they use a diction and syntax that is impolite, blunt, passionate, and sarcastic. Their language is of natural speech and dialect that makes full use of street talk and slang. By doing so, their voices resist the illusion of objectivity. They refuse to take on a disembodied voice. They desist from a poetic rhetoric that might confine, limit, structure, and render their words ineffective. Rather, these poets describe the effects of the violence and the threat of violence on their own bodies and lives, the lives of those close to them, and the life of their social and political world. Such acts decenter language and decenter individual words by calling attention to the discursive quality of language as both responsible for violence and the means for resistance.

Other poets in this collection borrow the language of the media to critique an institution that fails to represent them. These poets adopt the accessible language of reporting: a short, clear, editorial-voice that appears absent yet is highly personal and detailed. Ostriker describes this poetic language used for a media-oriented reader as "a pastiche of newspaper and newsmagazine prose styles" that "can provide a rope of credibility which fastens the poet's metaphor...to earth" (131). In these poems, media-language is significant because such writing reinforces that this narrative is news.

> But you don't seem angry,
> *people say, not having seen me grapple a man// with words...*
> ~Minne Bruce Pratt (104)

Strategic Anger

In her study of women's bodies through Mikhail Backtin's concept of the carnivalesque, Mary Russo suggests that women are subversive when they fail to control their mouths, either through consumption or exclamation. Russo writes that this failure to control the mouth "is a more generalized version of... the vagina. Together they imply an intrinsic relation among female fatness, female garrulousness, and female sexuality" (37). In their analysis, Carole Oles and Hilda Raz mark out the parameters of the feminist literary movement in poetry, including feminist attitudes toward the female body as cited in poems written by women (4). They suggest feminist poets reject a patriarchal, conservative and traditional view of the female body in order to consider the body in new and subversive ways, a process which may involve rage at the recognition of such sexist depiction (6) and may take up mythic stories about women in order to challenge them (7). Poets in this collection do not follow the dictum: if you don't have anything nice to say, don't say anything at all. Ostriker examines the "explosion" of violence, anger, and polarization in contemporary women's poetry. She explains such anger articulates "a need which may indeed have been buried for three thousands years" (127). Likewise to describe such rhetorical tactics by the second-wave feminist movement, Kathryn Flannery notes anger can be deployed to "work out of (rather than to be swallowed by) the maelstrom of rage" (114).

With the stigma attached to women's anger combined with the stigma of victimization, women poets who rage against violence trespass multiple social norms. Not only are they failing to control their mouth by speaking about issues some people feel are inherently private, they stir up others with their audacity to be loud and hostile. Using anger as a rhetorical strategy runs the risk of isolating readers who take offense to the author's tone, but it can also serve to garner attention to the poet's message in a way that choking back bitterness and rage cannot. In her essay, Meg Schoerke examines the use of pathos in poetry, particularly the ways gender norms after modernism limited many women poets' expression and emotional range: "women poets, consciously or unconsciously, tended to restrict or qualify their tears" (79). Schoerke explains that women "not only lacked an accredited tradition but also confronted the timeworn equation of female sentimentalism with triviality, still tended to evade claiming tears, and favored open expression of anger, or else politicized weeping" (85). Schoerke suggests women poets wrote elegiac poetry but did so by voicing their "grief through fierce anger" (96) and thus, "anger became 'literary capital' for women poets" (97). This technique is not only revolutionary because we encounter it in a genre that traditionally eschews polemic, it does so because it shows that *anger* is an acceptable emotion for women to express about the violence they experience or perceive happening in their communities. When poets in *Women Write Resistance* use anger as a poetic strategy, they take up yet another tool to resist violence against women.

The tremendous power – such as linguistics have made it known to us – the power to use, proceeding from oneself alone, all language, with its words of dazzling sounds and meanings, belongs to us all.
~Monique Wittig (93-94)

I feel that writing is an act of survival. But there is more than my own survival that is at stake.
~ Janice Gould[8]

Resisting for Change & Poetry as Action

Poets in this anthology ask readers to act, to resist. The idea of the poets' role to legislate for a more socially just world is not a new one. "Poets are the unacknowledged legislators of the world" (322), writes Percy Bysshe Shelley in *A Defense of Poetry*. Shelley asserts that poetry's power is the power to rouse people into action: "The most unfailing herald, companion, and follower of the awakening of a great people to work a beneficial change in opinion or institution, is Poetry" (321). Milosz tells us how and why governments fear the poet, "whoever wields power is also able to control language and not only with the prohibition of censorship, but also by changing the meaning of words" (411). Similarly Jorie Graham explains, "In fact, one could argue that poetry's difficulty for some readers stems from the very source of its incredible power: the merging of its irrational procedures with the rational nature of language" (352). Poets in *Women Write Resistance* do more than survive, they resist. These poets resist though poetry the violence directed toward women from a myriad of places in society—the media, social institutions, intimate partners, family members. These poets resist as they seek change.

To be a resister is more than surviving violence because one has taken an active step to call into question the violent act(s) and to rally demands for change. In my reading, poets use poetry as the platform of power to make life better for all. Elaine Scarry suggests humans make the world or make sentience via the artifacts they create (e.g. a chair, a coat, a poem). Humans project the self into the artifact which is then projected out into the world. She argues that these artifacts are evidence of the human desire to make life easier or better for other humans. She writes, "anonymous, mass-produced objects contain a collective and equally extraordinary message: Whoever you are, and whether or not I personally like or even know you, in at least this small way, be well" (292). The poet (from *poiesis* "to make" in Greek) changes culture by adding to culture the made things of poems. Scarry writes, "...the poet is working not to make the artifact (which is just the midpoint in the total action), but to remake human sentience; by means of the poem, he or she enters into and in some way alters the alive percipience of other persons" (307). Women poets who address violence strategically are resisters because they resist the way things currently are. Poems in *Women Write Resistance* remind us that poetry is action, poetry does something, or at the very least, has the *potential* to be. Neruda explained in his 1971 Nobel Lecture, "I believe that poetry is an action, ephemeral or solemn, in which there enter as equal partners solitude and solidarity, emotion and action, the nearness to oneself, the nearness to mankind and to the secret manifestations of nature" (105). Poetry can affect the larger world. Lorde explains that poetry is hope in action: "Poetry is not only dream and vision; it is the skeleton architecture of our lives. It lays the foundations for a future of change, a bridge across our fears of what has never been before" (*Poetry*, 370). Poems in this collection remind us that violence against women is common, a community issue, and not some secret—something of which to be ashamed. Because gendered violence doesn't affect the individual alone, poems in *Women Write Resistance* encourage readers to act.

WOMEN WRITE RESISTANCE
POETS RESIST GENDER VIOLENCE

FROM CAUTION: AVOID GETTING IN EYES OR
FOR EXTERNAL USE ONLY

      1.

Can't stop, he said—

          the kissing
was what mattered, not the stopping

or the idea of it, but

        that you needed to think of things
        in these on / off patterns.

6.

He's always kissing / responding.

  9.

And the screen door slamming
over its own squeak.

       10.

Like the bandage that clots
blood, closes wounds

          (without stitches:
          hair & twigs
          snarling nests (n)

The poem in relief.

12.

The story   (bird)
swallows
a lump   (fish)
in its throat.

19.

He hit you.
            You split—

Grandma Ellen Tells it Like it Was

Back then
there was no Crisis Line,
no Friendship Home to take you in.
You had made your bed, and there you would lie.

So you acquired the proper downward glance,
learned just the right brush strokes
to keep the picture pretty.
And when his heel came down
you did what you must
and kneaded your rage
into a hard round ball.
It was poison,
but it was yours.
You kept it tight inside.

There is no disgrace
in sleeping with the enemy.
You did it for the children.
You did it to survive.

And more often than not
he would die
first.

Rat

He sat on his gray haunches
at the chicken feeder,
sliding his jaws from side to side
slobbering up the grain.
My shadow shuddered across the floor and
he swiveled his head to toss me a glance,
then went on eating.
His eyes were red and insolent,
his scaly tail like a little whip.

Saturday nights when I was sixteen
a group of boy-men stood at the pool hall door
smoking cigarettes, smirking.
When my sister and I walked by, they slid their eyes over us
tossed their cigarette butts to the sidewalk
and slowly ground them out.

I went to the house and got the .22,
rolled the shell into the chamber.
He was still there eating.
I shot him through the chest, through the floor,
tossed him out with a shovel.
When William came, I was nailing
a tin can lid on the floor to cover the hole.

Rat, I said.

MEDUSA

She surfaced from Poseidon's rape alone
but for Athena plaiting snakes into her hair.
Who wouldn't want a face that turns a man to stone?

The most beautiful of three sisters turned
Gorgon, yet feeling human pain, there
in the temple where she fought alone.

Out of pride Perseus brought her snake head home,
wedding present for an exiled mother who, in despair,
needed a face to turn her consort into stone.

Think how the Trojan women moaned,
resisted being herded onto nightmare
ships, ravaged by Greeks. Not alone,

their children watching, plotting to be grown
to warriors or stunned by terror of what they'd share
unless they found a face to turn men into stone.

Think of any woman caught in war, in mundane
violence, atoning for her body's flesh and bone
praying only she might wake alone.
Why wouldn't she want a face to turn men into stone?

BLUE IS THE COLOR

That blue dress took her places,
flowered silk with three buttons
open at the top, ruffled hem. The way
it belled when she twirled in the mirror,
propelling her down a Paris runway
or fashion show in Milan. The way
boys looked at her when wind
pressed filmy fabric against her hips
and thighs. The way it floated up
around her waist when daddy came
to take his due.

VIOLENT ERUPTIONS

One year after your husband bludgeoned
the back of your head with a shovel
you still call this and his other attacks
volcanic eruptions. You still don't see
that his actions were within his control:
he hid with a shovel behind the maple
in my front yard in the dark
just waiting for our shift to end,
just waiting for you to climb out of my car
and walk up my walk
to what I thought was my safe haven.
I smelled him before I saw him -
piss and sweat and six weeks' worth of rage
that seethed through his pores.
I didn't see him lunge and swing
the shovel at the back of your head -
metal crunching bone -
just like he didn't see me fumble
for my six-week-old gun
and shoot him until
the tiny bullets
pierced him enough
to stop him -
like no restraining order
ever did.

CREOLE TOMATOES

> *Carmen Leona Reese, 17, a runaway and presumed prostitute, was one of the*
> *six people murdered in New Orleans during a 52-hour stretch in October, 2007.*

Early fall, the red natives turn
       soft with blossom-end rot. Each a small wound
           splitting at the corona. Inside, fruit
worms nest the seeds, fibers. The skin softens.

The girl left her home in Texas
       for New Orleans. She listened
           to the sweep of highway pass, watched
headlights slow, then stop.

In the fields, the tomatoes are placed in boxes
       or baskets. They are all overripe, decaying
           under the sun. One falls from the truck,
rolls off into a ditch. A bird begins its descent.

The bruises were too many to count. Each one
       overlapped the other: scarlet ovals
           around her throat. In the photograph,
her eyes were open. The bruises, black.

The tomatoes drop from the vines each day. The black-
       spotted leaves, heavy curtains hanging
           from the busted fruit. Grasshoppers
devour them within seconds.

So far from home and her body
       a ruined map. The sharp hook
           of a flashlight moved over bare feet,
a runner's calves, breasts, a weed-choked alley.

Bacterial wilt. Fernleafing. Yellow mosaic. The tomatoes
   open to heat, drought, late season. The leaves
     streak brown along the stems. Each leaf
a darkened shoestring. The fruit hard as a bone.

On Mandolin Street, the red flesh of sky broke above her
   nude body, above the gravel, the ants, the stained
     mattress in the garbage can. The star-
shaped wound at her temple, another in her chest.

TRAIFE

1

The word for food that isn't *kosher*—
beasts without split hooves,
who don't chew their cud
and anything from the sea
with no fins, scales or gills.
No one ever told me why, but
Mom said, "It's a sin to put *traife* in your mouth,
a sin, a bad thing, against G-d
and G-d punishes all sins."

2

The fear of G-d was in me then
and we kept a kosher home.
But my Aunt Eva and Uncle Benny ate
barbequed Chinese pork covered in a red goo
that made them look like bloody lips
and lobsters that were giant red scorpions
with bodies so tough,
you had to smash them with a tenderizing mallet
just to get to the meat.
I wasn't tempted to eat that stuff.

3

When Aunt Eva and Uncle Benny visited us
for a meal, we served the clean foods of Judaism:
chopped chicken liver mixed up with
hard boiled eggs and mayonnaise that looked like
greenish baby poops and was just as smelly;
fat torpedoes of gefilte fish with
beet-reddened horseradish that moved
like stinging ammonia up into your nose until
it felt like your face was all nose.

4
Once when my parents had to go out of town
to a wedding with no kids allowed,
they dropped me at Aunt Eva and Uncle Benny's.
It was dark and the stars were already out.
Walking to their front door, I could see
my breath rising to go live with the stars
and the night felt magical.
Uncle Benny ushered me inside, whispering
he had a wonderful surprise:
a midnight snack just for the two of us.

5
I knew about shrimp—
my best friend Joann's mom
sautéed it in virgin olive oil
with crescent moons of garlic
and a green dusting of oregano.
The shrimp cooked up so pretty,
innocent, white and pink,
sort of fluffy, looking like
tiny curled-up kittens
or maybe mermaids.
Could it be wrong to put something
that pretty in your mouth?

6
Exactly at midnight, Uncle Benny tiptoed
into the room where I was lying sleepless.
He had a white deli-counter container in one hand
and a bottle of Manischewitz wine in the other.

"This is baby shrimp," he whispered,
kissing my ear at the same time,
"for my favorite baby girl."
The shrimp were teeny tiny,
no bigger than a pinky nail.
"But, Uncle Benny," I protested, "I'm kosher."
"So am I," he said, winking, "100 percent kosher meat,
but you wouldn't eat me, would you?"
I giggled as he set the container on the nightstand,
and proceeded to tickle my chest.
"Look at these mosquito bites," he said,
pinching my nipples, and opening my pajamas.
"Let's eat the shrimp on top of kosher meat.
I'll lick it off you and you lick it off me.
Then every time something kosher will
be in your mouth, too."

It didn't sound right to me
but he said he'd go first,
and he did.

7
It's a sin to put *traife* in your mouth,
a sin, a bad thing, against G-d
and G-d punishes all sin.

Why I Dread Teaching *The Sun Also Rises*

When I used to picture the whole class, all fifty-six of us, lounging
    around a bar, sprawled under a fly-ridden
fan creaking overhead with a bartender listening like a burnt-out priest
    and a throaty half-lidded alto crooning to a mike,
I'd forget that always, even after I deliver my riff about World War One
    and life in the trenches where the guys
watched their buddies' brains explode into bloody pulp after wading
    for months in mud up to their knees, their navels,
one of the students, maybe Tiffany, will begin to whine that the book
    is disgusting, why should we care about no-good
drunks wandering around destroying their God-given bodies,
    and as for Brett, she's a total slut, the fact
that Jake loves her tells you how sick he is, and anyway, why do we
    always have to read such depressing novels?
Then Bryan will say yeah, she's right, and how come these dudes
    can afford to eat in all these pricey restaurants,
and even after William chimes in to counter that Jake actually has a job,
    Bryan will sneer, sure, he works maybe five minutes
between drinks—and it's uphill work to steer the class back on track,
    ask them if they've ever been hurt so badly
all they want to do is forget, but if I'm lucky it'll be William who pipes up
    again to say "Haven't y'all done Fiesta, come on,
you know how you party nonstop till you find out which of your friends
    are the real jerks, the serious assholes, and
finally you know the score, you're not fooled by anybody any more?"
    Maybe I used to remember the year when I traveled
with my cousin and a group of musicians, summer afternoons in Verona
    over a three-hour lunch before the concert when
the notes of Vivaldi flew to the dome of the cathedral and lived in my ears
    all the next day and the next as we ordered
Campari and soda before the evening's *passegiatta*, the long lounging
    at a round table as we watched the women and men
saunter and the *ragazzi* prance and the swallows lift above the piazza,
    swirl and dip while the sun dropped and the sky

turned rose, before a few of us found a little *ristorante* and ordered trout
        caught that morning from a stream in the Dolomites
where later we walked in meadows so far above the cars and smoke
        we thought we'd been lofted to a snow-glazed heaven.
During those months I forgot everything but the sweet tang of the air.
        But that's not the whole of it, not really the truth.
How I worked to forget the nights when my cousin was so drunk
        he made Mike in the novel look like a hero,
made Frances's sniping at Robert Cohn look sweet and kind, the way
        he'd yell at his girlfriend and call her "bitch,"
the way his hands would slide over the breasts and bottoms of women
        before they even realized he'd crossed that boundary
right out in public, and why nobody slugged him I still don't know.
        But then there was the semester when Guadalupe
perked up the class by saying that the novel reminded her of childhood
        in Monterrey, when her father took the family
to the Plaza de Toros on Sundays and explained why the *torero* wears
        a suit of lights decorated with gold and silver threads,
and how he uses the long skinny sword only for killing, how it's all a ritual,
        and that—just like Jake tells Brett—you're supposed
to focus on the bull, on every little movement, so it's not so horrible,
        it's like a ballet, a dance, though with death, and
so graceful it's kind of beautiful, but even so, she found it hard to see
        all the blood, and hardest to watch the horses.
The students were lined up in rows of unmoveable desks, and
        one of the fluorescent bulbs overhead
flickered on and off as the room grew quiet and nobody rustled a page.
        It's not so easy to spot grace under pressure.
I always wanted to be one of the insiders—not a whiner,
        sentimental, squeamish, like Robert Cohn.
When I taught *Lord of the Flies* to high school seniors, a couple of boys
        brought in a bloody pig's head dripping
in a paper bag, and I only said cool, where did you guys get that?
        These days I can't stomach anything stronger

than San Pellegrino after years as a Johnny Walker on the rocks
       wannabe aficionado, and I've never been in a war.
But I know how it feels when someone in a group, even in a family,
       goes berserk like a maddened bull, how it feels when
from out of nowhere, talk fired like a mortar shell explodes the head
       sitting next to you, maybe your own, open
down to the bone, with no one who can bring together the viscous
       edges of the wound, and you're so numb
all you can do is try to walk without stumbling, focus on the next step,
       the next drink, even if it's orange juice, because
this bull won't give up the ghost with a straight swoop of a blade.
       What you want is to go off alone and dive
into deep, clean water, start over with no carnage anywhere in sight,
       as if you could, and isn't it pretty to think so.

LUST AND SMOKE

You overwhelm me with your dress
always lifting, always falling.
Velvet parting, velvet portiere,
many callers (lifting, falling).

Many admirers admire
your velvet hallways and the silk
faux-Victorian settee
ribboned in scarlet and smoke.

How to compete with a tent so big?

Your dress hung from a tree,
your dress waving from a tower
and then your dress breathtaking on TV,
the reporter bleeding from her mouth.

All the people line up to see you
radiant in firelight, with shreds
of cotton in their fists
and their fists in their mouths.

The smoke is thick inside this tent.
And you, volcanic, spread.
Velvet ash, velvet wish.
Soon we are crawling. We are dead.

My Wife in All Things

My wife the sun. A chiffon dress lit with poppies and devilish hearts. Buttershine on a dinner roll for a dinner I missed. Her mouth salty butterscotch.

My wife the starlings. Their dust-black feathers and mouse-small faces stitched with stars. Skeletal legs threaded dark pink and jagged hopping that looks like joy.

My wife birch trees. The uranium factory near our apartment encircled by trees. Ash peeled to ash. Slender kneeling in the wind. A lace of burned fingers.

Wife hours, wife sleep. We dragged our mattress to the rooftop where the breeze was always night. Children quiet as ash. No light could be heard fanning among us, but the sirens circled our glass-dark heads.

Wife flesh, tender palace of the ears, tender net between shoulder and neck. A necklace of blood. Explosions overhead and the eardrums blow. She feels where blood falls and touches it. A red sound and its hammer.

Wife ribbon, knife, apple skin. She stayed red for months, hidden in my pocket until she puckered, a brown sack. I was the only one with a wife, an apple. My precious red love. This secret made me smile, even as the city wept.

Wife bodies laid out in rows with their eyes still open. Each one (not) my wife, wrapped in strips of white cloth. Her black moviestar eyes watch from the street, the newspaper, the television. Alive. Alive again, all the eyes hers.

BEARING WITNESS

For Jacki Phoenix

If you have lived it, then
it seems I must hear it.
—Holly Near

When the long-fingered leaves of the sycamore
flutter in the wind, spiky
seed balls swinging, and a child throws his aqua
lunch bag over the school yard railing, the last thing,
the very last thing you want to think about
is what happens to children when they're crushed
like grain in the worn mortar of the cruel.

We weep at tragedy, a baby sailing
through the windshield like a cabbage, a shoe.
The young remnants of war, arms sheared and eyeless,
they lie like eggs on the rescue center's bare floor.

But we draw a line at the sadistic,
as if our yellow plastic tape would keep harm
confined. We don't want to know
what generations of terror do to the young
who are fed like cloth
under the machine's relentless needle.

In the paper, we'll read about the ordinary neighbor
who chopped up boys; at the movies we pay
to shoot up that adrenaline rush—
and the spent aftermath, relief
like a long-awaited piss.

But face to face with the living prey,
we turn away, rev the motor, as though
we've seen a ghost—which, in a way, we have:
one who wanders the world,
tugging on sleeves, trying to find the road home.

And if we stop, all our fears
will come to pass. The knowledge of evil
will coat us like grease
from a long shift at the griddle. Our sweat
will smell like the sweat of the victims.

And this is why you do it—listen
at the outskirts of what our species
has accomplished, listen until the world is flat
again, and you are standing on its edge.
This is why you hold them in your arms, allowing
their snot to smear your skin, their sour
breath to mist your face. You listen
to slash the membrane that divides us, to plant
the hard shiny seed of yourself
in the common earth. You crank
open the rusty hinge of your heart
like an old beach umbrella. Because God
is not a flash of diamond light. God is
the kicked child, the child
who rocks alone in the basement,
the one fucked so many times
she does not know her name, her mind
burning like a star.

FROM WANTING A GUN

1. Nothing in the world

There is nothing in the world I want right now so much as a gun. A large gun, a shotgun. A shotgun with a sawed-off barrel, useful only at short range. A shotgun with a sawed-off barrel, useful only at short range but with a spread wide enough to completely destroy a man.

I want a gun, because they have guns. He had guns. Many guns, dozens, in racks and in cases. In racks above the bed, in glass-doored cases across from the bed. Guns you would see from the bed. Guns you couldn't miss seeing from the bed, even with your eyes closed. Even with your eyes blindfolded.

I want a gun, a shotgun with a sawed-off barrel, because he had so many guns, rifles and pistols and revolvers and shotguns, Oh, how he had shotguns—12 gauges and 14s and double barreled and single barreled and over and unders—and his special rifle, a Remington Sweet 16 (you're so sweet, oh sweet he said, stroking both of us, me and the gun).

His guns, his rifles, his Remington, his shotguns, in all their variety. Except a sawed-off short barrel. No short barreled shotgun, the kind that's useful only at short range, the kind that doesn't stop at maiming, the kind that gives a running target a fair chance, any chance.

I want this gun, a sawed-off short barrel shotgun. The kind that is useful only at short range. The kind that cannot maim or hobble. The kind with a spread wide enough to destroy all but the tiniest traces of a target. I want this gun, this sawed-off short barreled shotgun, then I want to stand and command, "Spread'em."

6. His favorite gun was me

It is easier to program a child than a VCR. Only three steps. Easy, time-test-
ed, ancient, a sure thing.

First, hurt the child. Hurt her a little, hurt her a lot, threaten to do more,
things she can't imagine. Since she couldn't have imagined what you've already
done, her own fear will now control her. She will blindfold and gag herself.

Second, explain to her over and over how she makes your violence necessary.
"If you didn't hate me so much, I wouldn't have to hurt ya. You could be
sweet for me. You could make this fun for yourself. But you don't want that,
do ya? I know what you're thinking, I can see them eyes. You wanna kill me,
so I gotta tie ya down tight. I wouldn't have to hurt ya near so bad if you'd just
be sweet for me."

Third, turn her anger against her. Take your gun, polish off your fingerprints,
put it in her hands, tell her it's hers, tell her the gun and her anger are the
same thing. "Ya hate me, don't ya. You wanna hurt me, you even wanna kill
me. You think you're so high and mighty, don't ya, missy. But you wanna kill
me, and that makes you just like me. You are just like me."

Three easy steps, and the prey is maimed and hobbled
and yours for life.
One, two—
the prey will blame herself,
she won't blame you.
One, two, three—
"you're a hunter too
if you hate me."

COMMON LAW

At first it was because the sex
was great and money didn't matter.
Because he said he loved you. And nobody
else ever had. Because you thought
you loved him, so when things got bad
you believed they would get better.

Because he wasn't always bad.
Then because he was all you had.
Then because of the baby.
Because he said sorry. And never again.
Because your mother said maybe if you tried
a little harder. Because your father said nothing.
Because you knew the neighbors were talking
and you wanted to prove them wrong.
Though they were right.
Though they never called the cops.

Because maybe you deserved it.
Because it wasn't all that bad.
Because he stayed (even though you dreamed of him leaving).
Because he said he'd kill you if you ever tried to leave.
Because you had nowhere to go
or didn't know how to get there.
Because you'd been with him so long
you didn't know what without him would be.

Because you'd forgotten how to imagine.
Because you'd made your peace with pain.
Because he was better than nothing.
Because everyone has their problems.
Because these things happen.
And when you ask yourself why
the answer is always because.

La Doncella

> *Eldest of three mummified Inca children discovered in 1999 in the Andes,*
> *exhibited at the Museum of High Altitude Archaeology. Asked where the*
> *mummies will be taken for display, the museum's director replied, 'Anywhere*
> *we can plug them in.'*
> —The New York Times

Dark is her head and bowed.
Legs crossed, arms held close.
In an acrylic container at 0 degrees she rests.
To see her you have to flick a switch:
If you don't want to see a dead body,
don't press the button.
It's your decision.
You can still see the other parts of the exhibit.

At any moment it looks as though she might look up
and fix us with her steady gaze
of reproach? forgiveness?
Her skin is dark and the scientists' white latex gloves
have carried her for CT scans, X-rays, DNA biopsy.
(Would they display their own dead daughters?
Make a headline of their grief?
Mummified Inca maiden wows crowds)

The female form has always been on view,
subject to the gaze of men
who claim what they want to take
by theft or force.
The perfect girl at just fifteen:
contained, immobile
thawable to touch.
Dead, non-white.

Yet science cannot explain how,
drowsy from maize beer,
she dozed with the others
then, stilled with chill,
in sacrifice,
joined their *ancestors*
and watched over their villages
from the mountaintops like angels.

THE CELLAR

I want my father to stop sending me down there
to fetch his daily gin, and potatoes for supper.
But there's no saying no to him, and no more places to hide:
he's found them all. Outside, the cellar's rusted door
stains my hands as I yank it open, scraping a branch
that whips back, grabbing at me — like he does.

Six stairs stop by a second door, with a hasp
and a slit between two thick planks. I press my face to it,
whisper to the bottles and potatoes: *Go away, I'm coming!*
But how can they? We're all dammed in this big
brick house in Antwerp, and I'm the *Kapo*,
I have no choice: it's them or me.

I kneel in the cellar, pray: *Don't let me separate*
families, don't let me kill a child... then inch
toward the shelves — and reach. Sometimes
I think I hear a moan, a sob; sometimes it's a child's wail
so exactly like mine I think it comes out of me — so I quickly
put the thing back: *I'm sorry, I'm sorry.*

The worst are the potatoes. I know exactly
how they lived before, rooted deep in wild, salted polders,
where lapwings titter between cattails and winds,
where rows of loam run past the horizon —
and here they are now, uprooted and cluttered in crates,
limbs groping for a wedge of light from a cellar door.

But then, from up there, comes father's call, weary, irked,
with that pitch and threat in the last vowel of my name.
I grab the gin, the potatoes, hold them as far as I can from my body,
run up, throw them on the table, and escape to my room
where I stand pounding my ears with my fists so as not to hear
yet another cry for mercy.

From My Window, I See Mountains

The morgue man pulls my father out of wall C:
the drawer so heavy he must brace his foot
against another one to pull it open. It jams
half-way, this is how far it will go: one half
available for viewing, the other no.

A voice cries out in the anteroom, then turns
into a wail so unbearable the morgue man leaves.
I'm alone with my father again. This time, I
lift the sheet further than allowed, and look.
This time, it is he who is frozen. And I see his

rage, down there, dark — like a fist
crammed between his legs. I touch his hands, the huge
Dutch hands that almost killed me, almost killed
my daughter, but once – on a shore in The Hague –
built me a sand castle, the morning after

his mother's funeral. It took him all day,
the deepest terror I remember, watching him
build that castle with the odd tenderness of brutes,
stroking the sand with weightless hands while I
sat at a distance, not knowing what to think,

what to do, Dutch rain sprinkling the sands
like a blessing. When the castle was done, he raised
moats around it, and mountains circling them,
while dusk wrapped us in its cerements, then night.
Not a word was uttered, even when we climbed the dunes

back to his mother's house, where I watched him
rock her wooden shoes in his lap, a hand in each
battered thing, the kitchen stove sighing.
After I buried him next to her, I flew back to this new
country, to this house surrounded by mountains,

with mountains around them. Some days, they seem
so quiet, so unchangeable, I think: shock, fissure, fault;
I want: chasm, quake, wave. But pray: plant me here
a while longer, plant this in me deep: nothing's perpetual,
eternity is only a word – kind as consolation, but as brief.

NO GIRLS WERE HARMED IN THE MAKING OF THIS POEM

No broken girl, blond girl, bloodied girl by the side of the tracks. No girl who
won't do the dishes, won't write, won't come unless she's in love. Can't even
hear the rain most times, can't breath. No kitchen knife, no back room. No
dirt fisted with a broken bottle inside her. Can't even watch the news without
some dead girl, red headed girl mucking up the works. Breaking open jars
of cherries in the parking lot. Won't swim, won't put her hands in the water.
Can't even go outside without swagger fastened to her hip. Won't eat lunch.
Won't set the bone because the hurt is too pretty. Won't write a word, a poem,
a book report on all this falling. A letter to her congressman in deepest pink.

MIDWEST GOTHIC

Say *mathematics* and everything comes loose.
It's written all over me in sequence,
the tire ruts, the trees fussy and ornate.

My voice sugars when I say his name,
fuck him beneath the arbor in his parents back yard,
all paper mache and chinese lanterns.

Today, it's someone's birthday. Today, it's someone's funeral.
I take away 7 eggs and still they seem to multiply daily.
Take lemon juice to my hair, lipstick when no one's looking.

It's a birthday. It's a beheading.
My name is four letters and a lisp.
A leaf in your palm that catches the wind.

Outside town, a woman once lay days beside
the road near the tracks, flies covering her like bandages.
She survived but I may not.

It's my birthday. It's a tragedy with cake.
There are five theories of blueness
and I proved every one wrong.

I can't keep dead girls out of these poems.
They knock on my door at 3am with a hangover,
looking for a match. One summer, my mother

locked us in the house and bathed us in milk
to stop it all from happening again and again.
Hoarded mattresses in the basement in case of disaster.

In dreams I stumble through the parking lot,
am shoved like a suitcase into a trunk
where I gag on gas fumes and ash.

I search my stomach looking for a mark.
No one likes to drive alone at night.

MARITAL PRIVILEGE

> *"In thin places, we become our more essential selves."*
> Eric Weiner, New York Times, March, 2012.

In Ireland they warn of thin places,
places with a sheer veil between this world and the next,
between bliss and despair,
between saved and damned.

In the soft light of a Dublin morning,
I feel my husband's hand
creep under my silk teddy.
I stiffen,
feeling the thud of refusal
over the tingle of yes.

Nudging himself between my thighs,
You know it feels good, he growls.

No, I insist, rolling over,
I hug the far-edge of the bed
not now…

He yanks off my panties,
unlocks my legs with a swift push,
shoves me to my knees.

I brace. Then a hurried
thrust, thrust.
When he's done,

he slaps my ass
and says,
Now, let's go eat.

He whistles in the shower,
I crawl out of bed.
Tug my jeans over shaking legs,
Paste on my smile.

The thin place between love and hate--
I have crossed over.

Don't

Don't know	*How Tuesday means he babysat* *Tuesday means her ma went out*
Don't picture	*Her breaking the bottle against her dresser* *Her taking shards in careful fingers*
Don't know	*How she stuck glass up in her* *Rinsed her hands in red red water*
Don't picture	*Him taking off his belt* *Hanging up his pants real nice*
Don't know	*How he put the music on* *Gospel loud and clapping hands*
Don't picture	*Her stare up to the ceiling* *Girl bed sinking from the weight*
Don't know	*How much he bled* *How the shards shoved in her*
Don't picture	*When he hit her hard* *Slammed her head against the bed post*
Don't know	*How she called nine-one-one* *How they never asked his name*
Know	*He never came back over*
Picture	*Her brand new bed*

Why My Mother is Afraid of Heights

When he held her by her ankles
        upside down off the roof   like she was

a bird he was plucking,   feathers
        flying in clumps through the streets of India,   like the dandelion fluff

from home   that you blew to make a wish like
        I wish he doesn't drop me   *I wish this hadn't*

happened,   this being   the molesting, the threats, then   -to come-
the disbelief,   when a girl came forward and said   *he made me*

touch him,   and she, my mother, said *me too,*   they told her she was
a naughty girl who just wanted attention,   like that was always

    such a crime, to want your parents   to look at what they had made,
what the body was doing, what   was being done to the body,   it was

too much to ask, and she   always was asking   for someone to
    love her, just   a little bit, and   they believed the first girl, who

must not have been held   over the roof, if she was telling,   she was older, heavier,
perhaps he couldn't   hoist her up and display her   like the Indian flag,

but when he held my mother   by her ankles   while below her, the open dumpster's
    mouth yawned,   spinning around,

waited to receive her body,   to swallow her up, this made the case,   she knew
    the bags of trash would not   cushion her fall, she was learning

at that very moment   the mass of her body   was immense, all sixty three pounds
    would plummet,   she was learning   to have a body

was a gift, to have a body   was to have a weapon,   was to
    be desired and that you could control   nothing, not even

which way was up.

HEAT

Desert washes make me think of dead girls
in shallow graves—lost—bereft of splendor

their sun-blonded heads turned to roughened dust.
Was this where Evil buried bodies back

in '66—would he go out this far
or are they harshly covered over now

with sprawl—the cheapened ground subdivided?
A deeper maul on top of stolen breath:

lives lived with dearth of yearning to escape
to shed fast the stench of cardboard boredom.

He stood before in a wash such as this
must have had an aftertaste of disgust

choosing already the better next one.
Then turned to go back past Lucky Strike Bowl

past Lube N Tune—past Factory 2-U
past Majestic Tattoo—past EZ Cash

past the Junque for Jesus billboard. Turned back
as I will turn on Escalante—stop

and wonder what those closest to me are
capable of that I have not yet seen.

I'M ONLY SLEEPING

Capitol Records thought the Beatles had no future
in America. Their *Somnambulant Adventure*
photo shoot—illusion and sex.

On the *butcher cover*: white bloodied smocks,
mock carnage of raw meat,
false teeth. Like *in the middle of a dream*,
glass eyeballs,
naked doll babies, their heads decapitated.

After its release, every copy
of the *butcher cover*
of *Yesterday and Today* was recalled
and pasted over—replaced to
avoid any possible controversy or undeserved harm.

Sometimes sex is just a bar crawl,
somnambulant adventure—controversy and harm

and when I have it, I want to
peel away the top layer, but
minimize the damage done.

BEFORE YOU

jumped my ex-boyfriend
punched the wall near my head
dropped out of school
quit your job
or said you'd kill
yourself if I left,

and long before you
forbade a ribbon for my hair
yelled when my contact slid out in the pool
or kicked our toddler's stuffed snow leopard across the room,

it was moonlight,
and you were handsome,
and we were in love,

and I was nineteen
and had sworn, after the trailer park of childhood,
never to let a man hit me.

I felt so proud of that rule I'd made up myself.
I was a leap into the future.
Bright and modern.
The Information Age.

      (You never did actually hit me,
      which made leaving stranger, confusing.
      You broke no rules. I changed.)

There was so much I didn't know
that night under the moon.

I'm so happy, you said, and you were.
Happiness lit you.
You make me so happy. I'm going to stop taking my medicine.

The world grew quiet.

Your new drug of choice,
I lay in the dark
and said in a small voice,
What medicine?

Land Grant

Oh, mama, the acid you threw
in my face was no actual
chemical brew. No druggist gave you
the poison you dripped,
drop by drop, in my drink.

But you'd have kept me from school
the way they keep girls.
Different god, same rules.
All I wanted was to think.

Why not deny me? It'd been denied you.
Instead of the thing you wanted to be,
you took to the skies, thin, pinned to "Fly Me!"

And they flew. Oh, they flew.

The dirty blade's in
the crone's clenched hand,
no man's,
when it scoops out the meat-nub of pleasure.

You made yourself
their tool, their fool.
You threw in your pain
for good measure.
I wasn't pretty, or neat.
Not a real girl, like you.

No matter.
You're old now.
When I fly through your city,
we don't meet.

When Dana Was About to Be Raped

I know what I'd do,
said my pretty, fair-skinned student
in her Abercrombie t-shirt,
in her clean, sturdy desk,
in response to the moment
in Octavia Butler's, *Kindred,*
when Dana is about to be violated
by a man she thought
she knew.
The two girls sitting
on either side of her nod,
their last minute ponytails swaying
in affirmation.

At the head of the classroom,
I wait for someone to say something
about shadows.
I can't help but see
the long, half-lit hallway,
hear the deafening buzz
of the industrial vacuum
the thick sensation
of someone behind me.
I want anyone in class
to say it doesn't happen like that.
To bring up the fact of arms,
twice the width of your own,
that draw the boundary
around your locker, the large hands,
bracing the solid bulk that leans
into your back. That smallness.
How you learn, that even though you
were always bigger
than your classmates,

able to throw home
from way back in center field, always
one of the boys
on the court, on bikes,
this mass of chest and stomach
pressing you flat exposes
how *female* you really are.
The breath in your ear,
the sheer blankness of fear,
it fills your brain like water
and you're drowning.
The tang of sweat in your mouth
is a gag. The words
you knew I'd be here
bind your arms.

*Yeah, I'd just kick him
in the groin and run!* She says
illuminated by the lights
of our well-lit classroom,
surrounded by the silent
mouths of her classmates' heads
bobbing in unison.

Teenage Lesbian Couple Found in Texas Park
with Gunshot Wounds to the Head
Portland, Texas June 24, 2012

It's always the girls   (we girls)
who mistake our heartbeats for hammers –
suffer their pounding when your kindness
insists it requires no exchange, & hush
their racket when a few rounds with Captain
or Jack change your mind, training us like dogs
to flinch every time you raise a hand.

It's always the girls   (we girls)
who wake up with more Adam in our step
than Eve, who weave back & forth
with intention, or wear our hair & lashes long
for anyone that is not you; who try *Pleases*, try tears, try Jesus
                    but still pop up in pairs along Colonial Parkway
                    & in Medford, our bonds made literal & eternal
                    in truck stop restrooms & along the Appalachian Trail.

It's always the girls   (we girls)
who assume we'll outlast your barbed wire
boundaries our bodies hurdle on the daily,
convinced our steel jaws will be found intact
when authorities, or archaeologists, unearth
each grave you chose for burying your rage
alongside our bodies, still intertwined.

SWALLOW

Your steady gaze,
The screaming,

      That time until my
      throat bled,

Swallowing the metal,
sweet burn,

      That time the hammer
      in your hand,

The steel claw swinging,

Your steady gaze,
My legs shaking,
My breath coming,
      faster, closer,

      In my eyes,
      The hammer swinging,

The only sound,
The neighbor knocking,

The water like acid,
Swallowing,
The air thinning,
My fists pounding,

Your steady gaze,
      The hammer swinging,

The steel claw, the blood
in my throat,

The light changing,
          My chest pounding,
          My breath burning,
          My face turning,

The blood, the sweet,
sweet
metal, my blood,
Swallowing,

The room spinning,
Your steady gaze,

          Your body moving,
          Our house clawed apart,
          The walls falling,

The blood swallowing,
          The hammer swinging,

The air thinning,
The blood swallowing, my

          eyes closing, my
          voice fading,

Your steady
gaze,
The truth, the
          hammer swinging.

I Wanted To Tell You The Dog Died

Your new wife answered when I called, I was crying
because of the dog, I could barely speak. I remembered
the day you came to say goodbye, eight years ago,
before I left town for good, and we took the dog for a walk,
acted as if we could be friends, which I hated.

But in all honesty, when she answered, I wanted
to tell her how that day ended, how we drove
to that dark parking lot, how you tasted, as you did
when we were married, of other women, and I wanted
to know if she noticed that too, when she was with you,
and if she felt the same confusion about that strange salt
on her tongue, or the same shame about sharing secrets
you worked so hard to keep. And now,

the dog has died.
Though we have not spoken since that night in the car, you
are the first call I make. It's late, but the dog, she was ours
for so long. I'm embarrassed to give your new wife my name,
to hear her angry sigh, and I'm embarrassed that I can tell,
when you begin to speak, that you are pleased, excited by
this sudden clashing of your new and old lives. It wasn't clear
until I told you, which I hated.

But you need to know that I wasn't crying because
the dog was some last connection between you and me, and
you need to know that I always loved the dog more than I
loved you. You need to know that I don't miss you. I didn't.
And, although I won't tell you, you need to know that
the dog didn't miss you either. She shit on the stairs when
you came to visit, growled at your voice on the answering
machine. But I had to tell you she was gone. I needed you
to know. Which I hated.

GOING TO SILENCE

I have decided to drive off forever through Autumn with all
I can carry. Through spooky-sad black and white movie light.

With my boxes and bags and bed piled into the back of a borrowed
pick-up - I have decided to leave him in the middle

of a hurricane while every front porch wind chime chimes
a miracle song to celebrate my going. Away from ugly Sundays.

Back toward myself - deeply altered - through the storm
to silence the beaten-down animal sound of my disbelief -

bruised and astounded - to silence my suffering in silence
and to silence his too-loud presence and my hope of surviving

his hands in my hair - to silence my hunger - I have decided
to drive off forever away from him through Autumn to live on

strawberry jam over toast with tea. I will be the fleeting
sound of a song he thought he heard, and moved toward, and lost

to a sky full of signals split by the wind. My hair will trail
and whip and tangle at seventy miles per hour - both windows

down. And in the morning he will find it all over.

After the Rape

You wore the same jeans for a week without washing them. You couldn't find a good reason to undress and your nude legs, wet twigs, threatened to snap beneath the weight of your bend. You switched from soda to warm tea. You wanted honey to bleed the roof of your mouth. This warmth. When a wasp landed on your forearm, you watched it for what seemed like hours. How it poised over you. How its stinger lifted, waiting. And you crushed it with two fingers before it entered your skin. You could not picture poison in your blood. When you tossed the wasp out the window, you imagined that it disintegrated mid-air, but instead it fell to concrete and you walked by it for many days after, aware of its rot.

A Grounding Against the Metaphysics of Morals

Or perhaps the story starts with books on her table. When the man breaks in, she's sleeping. Tomorrow: an exam. Tomorrow: a paper due. She's half-asleep, the sound of someone in the room soft as turning pages. First, he tells her, I heard a noise. By he is meant the handyman. And when there is no noise to hear, he bolts the door. He grinds her face into the wood. A cardboard box kicked. A hand bitten. That he will kill her if the night stays gray too long, a kind of a priori knowledge. He read Kant in prison, comics too black and white, dime store pulp too literal in its black and blue. There is an argument for anything, he says: to drown the small brown dog, to swipe the wallet, even to unlock the girl's apartment where she is falling in her sleep.

Schiller

Everything that is hidden, everything full of mystery, contributes to what is terrifying and is therefore capable of sublimity.
"On the Sublime"

The man with the knife is capable of sublimity. The man with the knife is capable. The man is capable of holding her in place. He holds her in a place called home. In a place called home, a man with a knife. In a place called knife, a man. In a place called man, a knife that splits the home from home. And later, it won't be a home to her. Will only be the knife, the man who holds the knife, the knife again. Always the knife again and the hand that holds the knife. In a place called knife, she's there, mistaking knife for night, and night for mystery. Everything a mistake. The shadow-body of a man can hold a knife. The shadow made by words can hold the knife, not very long, away from her. Away from her, the hand. The capable hand. The man in his sublimity. Away, the home no longer home.

Slippery Slope

I didn't stop that day—no time—
too fast—no place to turn around—
but the next day—on that ordinary
stretch—something pulled me over.
I climbed the slope to see it again—
the girl who looked eleven but may
have been older—fighting his grip—
the thin furious man—the long arm
striking her face. She was still standing—
after—my rear-view mirror told me.
No footprints in the slick grass—no blood—
just one glint—like a broken bottle.
A child's glasses with thick lenses—
intact—reflecting that day upside down.

FAME

His voice felt sticky; he whispered his name,
Paulie; he saw my picture in the paper, asked
– I didn't understand the word – Did I want him
to suck something. It was something
ugly – he was a grown-up stranger –
and I didn't know how to think about it,
couldn't answer, so without even saying
good-bye I set the receiver back
on its heavy black base.

                    When my mother
came home with her arms full of brown bags
and began unpacking Miracle Whip, Oreos
and Velveeta cheese, turning back and forth
from kitchen table to cupboard to fridge,
I stood in the doorway and sailed my story
into the room, except I couldn't bring myself
to tell her what he said. Slowly, she stopped
walking, stood still and turned the beam
of her full attention on me, something
so rare that my worst fears were confirmed,
and she said maybe I'd like to tell her upstairs.

We went up to her bedroom, where the gauze curtains
blew at the bay windows facing the street and
she closed the door, sat down on the bed.
I stood just inside the room,
forced myself to say the terrible words,
and I watched her face blanch – it must have been shocking
to hear such suggestions from a little girl with braids –
and she said yes, those were bad words indeed
and she said he was a very sick man, sick in his mind,
and she said that probably I shouldn't tell Daddy
the words he said, but she would tell him for me
and they would take care of it.

I felt so light,
as if I'd been carrying deadly poison
in a breakable bowl and had managed
not to drop or spill it, had safely
handed it over to someone who would
carry it up high, firmly, out of sight,
and who knew how to dispose of it
where I would never
have to see it again.

TRAGEDIES

I once saw a man on fire,
flames spreading from head to waist,
dermal tickling forcing a scream
too primal to explain,
yet he ran,
flames claiming more and more of him
until he was rescued by someone with a blanket
who hugged this human inferno,
then rolled with him to the ground

I once saw a woman in the midst of a miscarriage,
her body rejecting her heart's greatest desire,
her repeated "*No, No, No...*" decibels above
the hushes of nurses
who stroked her arms
and searched for veins,
hoping to quickly
rescue her from consciousness

I once saw a man grab his wife by her hair,
then drag her across a room,
his arms twice the size of hers
but everyone turned away,
eyes toward the floor,
ears deaf to her cries,
respecting the privacy of their public marriage

BACKWOODS

You'd go back to him, then,
your swaggering full-bird
second husband, fragged in Korea
and now hunkered down
here in this backwater?

How could you,
after he blackened
your eye,
dumb-bitched you
and wrecked your canoe?

You escaped from that place once,
his cottage collapsed
on the banks of that dirty, dredged ditch
he calls a river; all you needed was a car
where you could sleep, keep your things.

Yes, you're alone now we kids
are all grown and left home;
but would you really go back
to that tarpaper shack squatting
in bottles and weeds,

where your beloved canoe still lies on its side
split like your lip
where he kicked it,
the night you ran home to us
in your nightgown and only one shoe.

Bound Feet

Her own feet flat and wide, she dreams
of hummingbirds or orchids that men
might want to taste and eat;
she dreams the mince-step

and sway-back that deepens swell
of hips. She tightens the linen strips
across her daughter's instep arch,
looks at the arabesque shoe

on the shelf. She'd have beaten
her silent, but the girl was already
obedient, understood that nothing
inflames a man like

disfigurement or any other proof
of a wife's subjection; the need
to be carried by opulent litter
from place to place, how if

his paper house should catch fire,
she could not take ten steps
to safety but would burn, ash lotus
petals rising in a tranquil

watercolor sky; why she cradles
her child's foot in her warm, wide
lap and snaps each matchstick toe,
tenderly breaks each arch.

SONG OF THE RATTLING PIPES

Sometimes the house around her sings back,
oil heat clanking against the steel
in low industrial tones, a workers' march,
a miners' rag, muffled mutinies.

She answers, words drumming
their way into the plumbing
of her body, her veins a vessel for song,
blood-coursed vowels, consonance

carrying her up out of her body,
as if she were not pinned
beneath another's weight.
Steam whistles and spouts the melody

of her chorus: *A apocalyptic,*
B bayou, C cerebellum, D detritus—
she falls into the alphabet of possibilities—
F fallacy, G Galapagos, H hovering—

letters an incantation, a portal from her body,
rhythm lifting her up in a circle
of sound: *Z zinnias, A arabesque,*
B braille, until the house falls into silence, the lull
where the sun waits for the sleeping world.

FRANKIE SILVER AWAITS EXECUTION

In 1833, Frankie Silver became the first woman to be hanged in North Carolina after standing trial for the murder of her husband, rumored to be a violent alcoholic and philanderer.

When they first found me,
relief was all I had left to feel.

You see, there were always
two endings—and last year

I woke to both.
My husband went missing

and our daughter learned
to speak. All winter,

I swept ash from the fire.
I buried the axe.

I lived with the bones.
Neighbors searched the woods,

the house. I hid inside
my husband's clothes.

The nights are longer now
than I remember, the moon

and trees more restless.
The wind knows my reasons.

Don't tell me the monsters
my daughter draws aren't

sleeping beneath the bed.
Don't tell me forces

of forgiveness aren't
drowning within our veins.

Visiting the Ruins

Imagine the missing sounds.
A saltlick without the scuffles.
Stolid maples without their
raspy spray of leaves, dense
to the height of them. A child's
scramble.
        Then picture papyrus
or clay tablets or even this paper
blank, leaving not even a doodle
to be dug up, or a line, nor ring
of fieldstone to mark the quirks
and manner of the one who held
that instrument, quill or stylus.
Or pen. The fields plucked clean,
the parade grounds emptied,
all connections cut.
            Why else
does one write, but to deliver up
the vacuum and fill it. Not
to fix or finish, for what was
is sealed off and done, but to
wheel it out again on its own
cobblestone streets. And given
one's own slippery notions
of truth, to erect a stop sign
that says *here*:
        Here is the table
where the child drank her milk
and figured her decimals. Here
the arch under which soldiers
came, their boots ringing the stones.
And here in the weeds behind
the mechanic's shop, a child's
nightgown, tossed aside like
an afterthought of no account, as if
deeds were porous, and the gag
and thrashing legs were only smoke.

THE COST OF DARK II

My father first took me ice skating
at the Golden Gate rink.

Holding my hand, standing firm
when my ankles wobbled,

he walked flat-foot along the edge.
God would act like this,

steadying me, I thought.
Maybe not God—so often

angry. Maybe Jesus,
his gown cinched

by his left hand to keep
him from tripping. God

was quick to take off his belt,
crack it double against

his palm. God was a Rawhide
cattle driver, stampeding

us into the pen. Jesus
rambled with sheep,

letting them flow like tap water
around a rock or an automobile.

Jesus coaxed mystery
cats from under the bed,

let me eat ice cream
when God wasn't watching.

When God skated down
the hall to visit me

in the dark, the door
creaked a small cry. Jesus

had to close his eyes tight,
turn his face to the wall.

ATTIC SPELL

is the head of the house not
  the whole of the house where
the he is the head of the
  household. The head of the heart
of the wife is the heart of the head
  of the hold in the attic.
The wife in the attic, the hole
  of the house, is the throbbing, the heart
is aloud with the beating, the head is
  the mind, is the turning in rooms
of the house of the beats of the heart-hold.
  The chambers, the rooms of the house
hold the thoughts in the holdings,
  the held of the hiding in holds.
The head is the dead of the heart of the hold
  of the held in the head of the wife-hold.
The rooms of the wife are the he
  of the hold are the doors to the lock
to the attic. The wife is the turning
  and throbbing through seasons,
the reasons, the heart of the held home.

CONJUGAL TRIPTYCH

She fell in love only with men
she invented, shaped as we shape
infant bone, forged in and forced
from the womb, contracting red sinew
of that strongest muscle to which her lovers
always returned. She took them in, wondering
at catching trout instead of marlin in Barker
Reservoir, pissed they're trout.

The SAC pilot made her
Mrs. Wilson when she was seventeen,
made her wait all night in his black Corvette
outside a New York abortion clinic, drove her
to white-glove Air Force dinners, ordered
that she bleach her hair and not cook shit
like lobster thermidor, but follow his
mother's tuna casserole recipe. She
kept her hair dark and stopped
cooking, took to staying up nights so
he wouldn't touch her, after watching
him cram crisp dollars into a Tijuana stripper's
vagina at the Officers' Club in Del Rio.

She left him for a brief
conjugal interlude with a MAC
pilot who she refused to follow
to Korea, sighed, *Damn, if I added one*
from TAC, I'd have a complete set. Near
the end of a third marriage, gray streaking
her dark hair, she wrote a thesis, planted
aspen, contemplated the state of her
union, said, *Last week I watched my*
husband spit in our son's face. Next week
I'll drive that man to the Denver
airport, shoot him, leave his body in
the car, and take the bus back to Boulder.

FOUNDATION

As I sponge on my Clinique
High Performance makeup
I mark the markings on my face.
Fine lines announcing themselves
like uninvited relatives
who will not leave the house
of my skin, instead dig deeper
because they plan to stay
until the last supper.

Yet, I'm told my skin's still smooth,
soft as yesterday,
still can turn a head
not a headstone,
still can show my female verve
with glow and flush.

Blemished, but unbruised
unlike the skin of women
who have known fist, hand,
knuckle applied
to their flesh,
who tried to hide more
than make up,
their made-up
stories
of falling downstairs,
falling
for the wrong guy,
staying
for the wrong
reason.
Women always falling
out of themselves

like shooting stars
that explode
in a shower
of hot white
pain.

Pens and Cellulite

So much of my pain
(Broken hymens amid threats
bruising tender young flesh lips
wrists held down…)
is written over in successions
of absence, pieces hacked away
expelling diseased grief.

Pain written skin. Story of Indians & Creoles. Victims and those who refused
to lay down in the everyday disobedience of survival. I am a narrative of
progressions, removals and returns, raised in keloids and rivers of stretch
marks. My body has become an exercise in cartography.

So much of my emptiness
(Loss of your words,
absence of your hands,
faith in myself)
is filled with cellulite
dimples refusing
ice cream in favor of
late night talks with
caste shadows.

I've sought to re-inscribe story on flesh. One of love and survival—scratched
and injected under vibrating pen of tattoo gun. It is broken in its narrative,
disturbed by rolls of soft flesh I have yet to pen a story of affection for…

Rape's ghosts taunt violently
scraping glass edged memory
till I am fat girl laughing to quiet
pain. I've danced across the country
keeping time to history of lies,
treaties, oppression, and children
filed away into schools.

I traded in scissors and knives for needles of ink and computer keys. Pens leaving trickling trails of blood— on flesh and cyberspace. These pens carve rivers of wanting, release, adoration, voice and self. These pens raise startling images of color against open spaces of fleshy leaves of paper, in a map of opposition, resilience, and arias alternating betwixt strength and fear.

The pens of my mothers
are dipped in pain spewed from
years of holding up sky
(when others sought to let it fall…)
My mothers write across imaginations
Of men who thought cutting their tongues out
Would mean silence.

And like the mountains and valleys of our mother
I am vast, dimpled and rolling—
Read me like brail.

FROM WOMEN ARE TIRED OF THE WAYS MEN BLEED

Four

> *Can hearts be at peace*
> *when marriage and war*
> *become identical experiences?*

Women are tired of the ways men bleed
by breaking open
other people's veins.
firemen are brave souls
policemen are brave souls
soldiers are brave souls
and housewives
housewives are brave souls
let us respect the bravery
of housewives

during the Vietnam War
and during the Iraq War,
in the u.s. more housewives and girlfriends,
more brides and mothers
died at the hands of angry husbands and boyfriends
than u.s. soldiers died in the Vietnam war or in
the Iraq War.
These have been violent periods
for soldiers, housewives and girlfriends.
I don't mean to disrespect soldiers
for their sacrifices
I mean let's honor housewives
as soldiers
in the evolution
of marriage   embedded
in the evolution of war
as the primary initiation rite
for sons, for husbands, for fathers

war is a kind of marriage

Marriage, for many women, is a kind of war

saying "I do" enlistment for
the most dangerous duty, the frontlines
of the husband-centered family
the frontlines of punching bag duty
"honey wontcha be my punching bag"
wontcha catch his emotions
with your face
wontcha let him twist his feelings
around your neck
wontcha put your body between his
expressions of rage
and the children

Do the brides know, like soldiers, do they think about the odds
the way soldiers talk in the training barracks,
what they say packed together in the truck beds on the way to the front?
Do they say to their friend at the bridal shower,
"I might not come back from this."
Do they say to their families, "Send me your love and your courage,
let me always come home when I need to, and don't forget to
put a white cross on the road.
don't forget to put a white cross in front of the house,
don't forget to put a white cross somewhere if I—
if I don't live through this marriage."
Do they whisper to the bridesmaids, "I don't really know him,
what is the family history of violence, what does his
mother say about her life
secretly, to herself?"

Do the bridesmaids answer, "You might not get
through this, he might turn on you the second year,
(as happened to J.)
after the first child, he might kick you in the stomach
(as happened to V., as happened to M.)
during the pregnancy, he might break your nose the first time
you say no to anything, (as happened to D., as happened to R.)
he might never allow you to leave him,
stalking you for years. (as happened to L., as happened to N.)
Does she look in the mirror at the dress fitting,
say to the woman pinning her hem,
"What does he know about himself
that he keeps secret?
What does he not yet
know about himself
that he will learn after he reads
my body as a book?
after he writes on me
the script of his emotions?"

SONG, AS SOLUTION

In old rural villages in South Africa, women gathered to create a song about an abusive man and sung it openly until he changed. These songs were known as "women's play things."

They sing how rage felled the moonlit evening

>> where exactly it was
>>> she first began screaming
>>>> that shook the pretty stars –

>> how his arms lifted   precisely
>>> to lower   her body

> and of her flung body.   They sing also

of a long silence which came
>> from their mud & wattle hut

the following day
and of the next day too, they sing

how it first looked when she appeared

>>> barely

>>>> walking

a bruise
 darker than skin
  on her body   still weeping still raised,
            they sing

with bushels balanced on top of their heads
>> a steady song of him

deep into African fields

where he is
slashing to bring down the husks

and continue even   while fists   of sun
light
beat
about

until a blushed shade of dusk brings him homeward
in shame.

FOR ALL THE WOMEN

This is for all the women
who live in fear
who are warned not to walk alone
whose nightmares spill into the day
whose feet turn to stone
who are abducted tortured dumped in a field

whose dates take advantage
who say No but aren't believed
who are afraid to ask for a condom
who risk HIV/AIDS
who are slipped a drug into their drink
who must prove it was "forcible"
who hear him swear it was consensual
who drop charges rather than relive

who are bullied at school
who are too young to know it is wrong
who tell someone who doesn't believe her
whose father brother uncle cousin family friend would never do that
who run away but are sent back home
who bear the child from incest or rape
whose abusers go free
whose own mother disowns them

who are intimidated
who are neglected or deprived
whose husband lover acquaintance takes advantage
who endure the trauma the words
who witness cruelty to animals
who try to shelter the children
who are afraid to seek care counseling testing treatment

who know it is coming
who are afraid when he walks through the door
who feel the fist the hand the boot
who are slammed into wall bed floor
who are made to believe it is their fault
who stay with him because there is nowhere to go
who cannot tell anyone

who were publicly flogged drowned burnt
who at birth are unwanted abandoned killed
who are not reported missing
who are never found

who are denied an education
who have no voice or voting rights
who need permission to work
who are not allowed to drive
who cannot leave the house unaccompanied
whose flesh cannot be seen
whose genitals are mutilated
who suffer acid burnings
who believe it is God's will
who rely on hope and prayer
who must obey the elders
who are property of their husband father family
whose husbands are allowed to beat them
who are forced to marry before menstruation
who must marry a man with multiple wives
who become sexual slaves
who find a boyfriend on their own
who are stoned to death for family honor

whose village is invaded by soldiers
who are gang raped or raped with objects
who are held down while they take turns
whose husband brother children are forced to watch
who are scorned blamed rejected and the children born to them
who flush their fetuses down the toilet

who are powerless against corporate pollution
who live in dangerous neighborhoods
who know the dealers the pimps the prostitutes
who go to bed hungry most nights
who endure schools below the poverty level
who drop out of school to work
who are kicked out of the house
whose husband boyfriend lover abandons them and their children
who are told it is their fault for receiving welfare
who are told they are lazy
who have no health care or child care
who work multiple jobs to put food on the table
who stand in line for the children's food clothing supplies
whose absent fathers are not held accountable
whose absent fathers are in jail
who were brought here illegally as a child

who sleep their way to the top
who injure themselves when they hit the glass ceiling
who work the same job but are paid less
who are denied promotion because they "can have a baby"
who endure sexual harassment
who fear retaliation
who are expected to accept lower wages
who support the farmers policemen firemen
who fed and danced with soldiers on the trains
who maintained the home front built the bombs welded the rivets
who were fired when the men came home

who know they are different
who are born this way
who choose to stay in the closet
who live with discrimination
who do not have legal rights
who are taunted scorned beaten

who are told they are not smart enough
who are too pretty not pretty enough
who are ashamed of their bodies
whose breasts are too large or too small
who are told to dress more modest cover up stay home
who are treated like objects
who pose or pole-dance because they need money
whose bodies are prized for male pleasure

who are not allowed to control their wombs
who are dumped at menopause
whose standard of living plummets after divorce
who are cut out of his will
who are replaced with trophy wives
whose men are just being men
who bristle at the word feminist

who blow the whistle
who report their injuries
who train the police
who answer the hot lines
who treat the victims
who provide shelter counsel support
who fight back teach prevention
who know what is best for their own body
who warn believe protect the children

whose fathers love them
whose men respect them
who empower other women
who speak for the environment
who share their wealth
who stand up for their rights
who come out
who change the laws
who stop the civil wars
who raise the grandchildren
who break the cycle of violence

who speak
who listen
who believe
who survive

For all these women, and
for all the world

OFF

He's off, he's really off, he's so far off
he'll never come down, been off for a
week now, no, two weeks, the water's
deep, he's so far gone he'll never come
up, he'll probably be off the rest his
life, off to Omega and no insurance.

I'm off too, she said. Outtahere–off, if
he comes home oiled again. Get off of
me, she said, I mean if a man is going
to act like that, I'm gone, away, off the
shelf, absentee, off before you off me
off like a sock, you're off your rocker,
you know that? Off your nut. Off
your trolley, call 911.

That's way off, he said, just because
I'm off the wagon doesn't mean I
don't love you no more. Oh yeah, she
said, Oh yeah, he said, and he took off
his shirt and cuffed her.

I'm off, she said, I'm really off, and
she should have gone, she should have
gone.

FROM SHAPINGS

ii.
What if when, barred with furniture,
the bedroom door
still bulges from blows
landing like bombers on P.T.s
when the world is at war.
And on the other side
he pounds, pounds,
pounds bloody wrath.
Rage fuming from terrible bottles
somehow impounded
behind his brow.
And then if ampules burst,
shattering, releasing fresh
adrenaline into fists,
I think she must be leaning
her back into wood,
hands over ears, numbing.
The quaking from blows
shaking her into a crumpled mess.
Late at night,
a stainless steel shelf
might glide her
back into a drawer.
She could be in a basement
with morticians circulating,
almost arctic breeze blowing.
Their scalpels rocking on tables
wheeled back and forth.
When I envision this, something spinning
gyrates past blue coated lab
technicians, green sheet draped nurses.
Everywhere, blood drained bruising

blends with autopsy marks.
Formaldehyde petrifies her soft
flesh into metamorphosized rock.
Not far away, a marble stone
lies snugly between
green grass blades.

No, I am not a Vet
Quincentennial Poem, 7-7-92

Closing, closing long, still,
desperately   trying to rest
my eyes   my visionary
statement   rise
there arises   times
clips, flicks, changes
in time   slipping
back   in time   back
false   film effect
strobe   see
remember white
men   white, white
men killing women,
children,   killing Indians,
and men   Indian men
trying desperately   to
kill me,   our own
men,   reacting reaction
action to oppressed
oppression repetitive
it   throws back my
face, my heart   slides
down and forth up my
bladed back, crawls
up scratched parched
listless tongue quickening
relapse tendencies
"But I didn't do anything"
and they proceed to
maim   killing thousands, to
turn back on   one   survivor,
this precise second   in
replay   evolves repeating

dream   blows to
the frontal plane
guard my 3D existence,
terrorizing women, children,
bayonets slicing   into
tiny warm bodies
beaded flags on
sacred heads   and wisdom
all ages   in their beautiful
black eyes   turning over
and back   in regard to
overwhelming constant
batter and mix whip–
lash   to certain refrain
feel dangling effect rabbit punch
to rubber   punching bag
my head   my point
conceptual   conception
thought process shield
and emergence place
I feel you reaching
through   aiming not
at me but deeper
through–behind me
to the wall you
collide   your jabs and
hooks into my skull
protruding damage
through   object resting
above my bladed back
neck snap cheekbone
thrash   eyes no longer
have clean form but
swell beyond recognition

senseless I am suspended
yet standing   out cold
yet balanced on locked
knees   as you   purse   your
reaction action   to the oppression

bestowed upon us
as a people   your anger
confusion   images
infants, women
our grandparents,   theirs
being mutilated   so
you mutilate the mother
of your children
grandmother of your grandchildren
drop the bomb–oppression
upon her   that is

was me   breaking parts
spirit   breaking my
spirit irreparably for
as long as I exist.

The Art of Exes

Twenty-three years old and I'm bracing the door,
though my love was strong enough to cleave
the deadbolt, though his touch meant bruises

secreted in long blouses, shoulders struck
the color of wild strawberry. Nineteen
and the boy I'd given my virginity is home

for summer and I won't take off his sweatshirt,
because his grandmother found him
overdosed on pills, called to say she's sorry,

his face is still beautiful, the surge of tantrums
she'd rocked him through as a baby finally
redeemed his sleep. And now, when the dark ruse

of your ex-wife is everywhere, I think of her
hair in the last photo you have of her—
it was sun-smothered blonde, stunned by light.

She must know how the body you built
together refuses to yield; intimacy is its own
heredity. How the stun stays on until you

own what you love. When I close my eyes,
it's teaching my body. I close my eyes and still
feel their hands.

Pulp Nonfiction

He has stepped from a dark waiting place. He has moved toward her body with the crude insistence of a bad plot.

Her mind is stopped. She is fixed in the wisdom of stories learned too well: Be calm. It is inevitable. Do not struggle. He will only hurt you more.

For one long moment she stands mute, without motion. She could die of suspense. Then (here's the reversal) her pen is in her hand and stabbing through his flesh.

Unhappy ever after, she will live to confess how the fury in her throat exploded red and harsh and howling.

This story, like the others, is ugly and raw. It speaks a kind of wisdom. If I ask why we have such stories, such wisdoms, will I breach some artful code? Will I violate some expectation?

CLEAR LINES

1.

"That's because of you," Jbo says, "He can't bear to not see you. That's how good you are."
Jbo says this right after I tell him about how Jimmy's been stalking me. So, then it's my
fault, in a good way though? Like I'm so good he can't let go? This explains all the fishing
line tugging at my parts, soft pyramids of skin. Every boy/man leaves in his hook, then he
fuckin' reels me in forever and the hooks won't come out. Unless they rust off. This could be
years. This is my problem. I'll swim alone.

2.

A captive dolphin lives urgently, like sperm hits walls.
The dolphin cannot escape. Can you imagine heads bleeding?

This is a rehabilitation tank! You see the scratches on their backs,
the whites against the gray?

This is healing time. This is exercise time. Watch them jump high!
and fall down into a treat.

They don't tell you that rehab lasts forever. Movement under still
chlorine. Ripples rise like fat, squished and stuck.

The dolphin tries to die at the bottom of the pool.
I must take naps.

3.

Turns out Jbo wants to fuck me too, he shows me his rod, fishing rod, that is. His line ready,
bobber and all. Turns out that's what he wants. Probably even while we surf. Or talk about
music. Or smoke. Or talk about Jimmy.

4.

I swim in the quivering tank too. The dolphin's head bleeds, waters red:
both of us requiring sea, but sealess.

LIGHTS!
(A NIGHT WITH THE MISFITS)

> *[Montgomery Clift's] the only person I know who's in worse shape than I am.*
> - Marilyn Monroe

"Diamonds are a girl's best friend," but they don't save her as they drop down her face, smearing paint. The driver tries to catch them, stash them for his pocket or fly. All men drive drunk. All men drive drunk. All men drive drunk. The blonde bombshell chants gently to herself. She swims in fluid on the rocks, dodges iced constellations, waits for the ride to end.

While she dances with an Oak tree, her arms are clearly woman, despite her piggy tail attempts. The recent divorcee sits quietly, then talks about dancing interpretively, dubs Arthur Miller's voice. Montgomery Clift bites his finger, as seductively as Marilyn. Eyes divert to him. The pair's tumblers melt tulips. Their hips close in. They swallow the tulips and chew.

"I don't like the way they grind women up out here," Montgomery says. Marilyn's knees seem dark in the dirt, her white shoes, filthy under star light. They crookedly hug. Their lips too full and soft for society, sip. Their eyes— crystal vases full with water and sunrise, await flowers. His vodka and grapefruits say to her, "you got such trust in your eyes." She whispers, "it's the Nembutal."

Clark Gable rolls on the ground, plastered—a temper tantrum. He argues belligerently, "didn't your papa ever spank you and then pick you up and give you a big kiss?" A man's pain is erotic. Like her cheeks, cherries and nipples. The foggy dust whirls about her moist face and lashes; diamonds stamp roadways. A large gloved hand muffles Montgomery. Blackness.

She screams out, "murderer!" Her feelings spray bullets at households.

She catches a ride home from Clark. He promises to love her.

BACK THEN

I can't picture the first time I saw dad hit mom.
Her shriek meant she hit the floor.

I heard him whip big brother outside my bedroom.
Beat up sis who fought and called dad nigger.

We called her crazy. Later she skinpopped speed.
Her schizophrenia came out. The voices.

One day we were arguing over Monopoly.
Dad walked in, mad at his losing horse.

Snatched a broomstick and hit me. I kept quiet.
But I see it pretty clearly now.

MOCKINGBIRD

That mockingbird could make me paranoid,
the way he's always got his eyes on me
(as if he were a cop in unmarked car)
from hidden stakeouts in the dogwood tree.
He wants to be the first to grab the chunks
of desiccated fruit from millet seeds;
like Pavlov's dog inside a feather-suit,
he's learned that I appear before he feeds.
I wonder, does he ever take a break,
relax his vigil, watch the butterflies?
Some nights I wake and shudder in my bed,
imagining those fixed, unblinking eyes,
or flash back suddenly to 21,
a pretty girl in crosshairs of a gun.

POMEGRANATES

My mother, gray bird
beside a white bowl
of pomegranates.

They flare
against her face,
creating an odd
balance.

She is retelling the family
myths. In this one, her mouth
is cut and bleeding, her teeth
pop out like seeds.

It is winter.
My father is King
of the Underworld.

"My whole mouth,"
she explains, drawing open
her lower lip, exposing the hidden
scars, "was pulp."

I memorize exactly, word
for word:

*He was quick
and strong, his punch
like a boxer's.*

*We'd been married
only six months, still newlyweds...*

as I pluck a pomegranate
from the bowl, hack it

open, place

a single blood
red seed on my tongue.

WHISKEY NIGHTS

He was still human
but he grew guttural and cruel.

Even asleep
he would thrash at us and howl
like a wounded animal.

What was it that tore
his insides?

Once he wrapped himself
in an electric blanket, plugged it in
and stretched out on the wet grass
"to watch the stars."

We prayed he would
electrocute himself.

(Dear God, those howls—)

Those were our moonless nights,
love at such low tide we felt death
was the only possible future.

When the priest offered
the blessing at his funeral, I saw
a light in the shape of a man rise
out of his coffin and walk
soberly toward me.

HOME SECURITY

After the installers leave, I sweep sawdust from the floor with a rag.
      A paper with instructions: to disable, type code backwards
          plus secret sequence: *disarmed—ready.*

I met my first thief at fifteen.
      He tooled my body to lockpick his conspiracies.
          An inside job that took five years.

If red light heartbeats on the screen:
      armed—away.
          Exit now.

He didn't have to hold me down. *Tell me you like it or I'll make you bleed.*
      I'll make your mother bleed.
          My own codes and sequences a mystery to me.

I try to trigger the motion detector with treebranch arms—
      not tall enough.
          It's For Your Peace of Mind ™.

After the pain was over he said
      you are strong, very strong.
          I felt my heartbeat in my neck each time.

Disarmed—I bite my lips, fingers. Easy to bleed me.
      The first time, I called out: a child's voice
          god-virgin-mary-help-me.

Second Thief, MD wrote *Patient resistant. Increase antipsychotics.*
      [She blesses the bathroom before her bath.
          Runs salt along all her exits.]

Tonight I hunch near the living room window in the dark.
      Wall mounted keypad glows light blue, like
          a Virgin Mary nightlight. If I unlock my own knob,

a barrage of beeps. Female voice: *alarm front door!*

    Disarm now! Disarm now!

                No exit from my safety cage.

My own voice wakes me in the dark:

    you'll never be ready.

          I rob myself again and again.

GIRL ON GIRL

Circle me and say, We can't fight girls.
You intend me to battle
the woman descending the stairs, want her
mace and my sword
to clash midair.

My catsuit's tighter than skin.
Her plaid schoolgirl-skirt's short enough
to expose Eden in white panties.

Hope we miss major arteries
for a few rounds,
shout, Give us a strip tease, baby,
imagine a slice here (a snicker-snack there)
and a pert nipple will pop
from fabric slashed in all
the right places.

But this time, we don't swallow
the bait. Before your lust reaches your pants,
we're back to back
and our weapons –
bigger than yours incidentally –
point towards your smirking faces.

Assume you can take us.
Metal flies so fast
your arm's on the floor
before you finish rolling your eyes
at our naiveté.

INANNA IN IRAQ

I'm the goddess of heaven and earth,
and this is my Mesopotamia.

The Tigris and Euphrates
pour out of me.
My navel's a primeval sea,
my ovaries, syzygies.
So, you wanna fuck with me?

I'm Inanna
behind the eight ball.
Try me.
I'm Inanna
behind the enemy lines.
Find me.
I'm Inanna
behind the conspiracies
behind the green door.
Open sesame.

Let me tell you about my vagina
as a bomb site.

Let me show you
what's behind the black veil.

Shrapnel in my labia,
my clitoris a burning hole.

Lying on a meat hook
in the depths of Abu Ghraib
my eye sockets raw
with tear gas
my vagina erupting

blood and pus
from endless cycles of
broom handles, penises and gun barrels.

What goddess
in her right mind
would stand for it?

My vulva
swollen with shrapnel
My mouth
retching vomit and vengeance.

Don't call me victim.
Save that for a hundred thousand dead.
My third eye's Babylon.
My tears do not spell
victimhood.
My tears are floods
covering Hummers
with oil and blood.
The earth is my ally.
I put my ear to the ground
and hear my own heart thumping.

This is my Mesopotamia.
Who do you think you are?
Ebih, Mr. Mountain God?
I'm Inanna
the axe-swinging mama
flattening mountains
till your lips kiss the dust,
singing my praises
to my father, the Moon.

I tell you,
I am bearing witness,
bearing soldier after soldier
faster than your country clones 'em.
Don't like the way I'm talking?
Should have bombed my mouth,
but no...

If your vagina
was a bomb site
do you think
you could talk about it?
Or would you dare
to move content beyond words
like pages of bullet holes
oozing spectacular
meanings,

like confetti
upside down,
like pottery shards of
"No!"

In Praise of a Co-worker

Thank you in advance for your attention to this matter.

Thank you in advance for expressing interest,
for any cards or gifts you may deliver,
for answering my questions:

*Why, on a business trip, did our regional manager
drink too much then moan my name outside my hotel room?*

*Should I have called for help after his tenth text message
asking if we could cuddle?*

Thank you in advance for your prompt response
and for being as specific as possible.

Thank you in advance for helping me understand
that if I report his behavior to Holly in Human Resources
she might never contact him,
or that although he was named "Team Player of the Year"
at yesterday's meeting, you think he's a jerk.

Thank you in advance for your expertise:
perhaps this also happened to you
and taking breaks to blast music in your car calmed you.

Thank you in advance for assisting this work-in-progress—
my smile, stirring to life at your voice.

Portraits of Marriage

1.

Take off that veil.
I want to see the sun strike
your maggoty little face.

2.

I wear my husband
as jewelry, finger bracelets
inked in vivid yellow, purple,
brown, back stippled
with the shuddering kiss of belt strap.
For these love tokens, I give myself
in return: one tooth, crown cracked,
swimming in a mouthful of blood.
My tongue presses
into empty expanse, measuring the loss,
the budding cavern my veil must fill.

3.

This knot of flesh
cradling hip bones rise, like dough
kneaded and stretched
into pleasing round loaves.
My husband's knuckles pummel,
hoping that I too will turn
supple and pleasing.
Or if not me,
then the lump of son,
sipping blood in my stomach,
trembling for his father's embrace.

The Accident

I had no business there in the first place–
I'm putting on weight—but the counter help was all smiles,
Having survived the lunch hour crush. My husband and I
Ordered burgers and fries; I was in front, so I chose
A seat on the far side, back to the window.
I picked off two thin rings of onion; the fries were limp.
We were talking about some recent trouble,
Something about the car, maybe, both of us
Interested, me a little bitchy, so it was almost the way you turn
Instinctively, say from a spider web in a darkened hall,
How I looked across the restaurant and found her face,
Left cheekbone swollen to a baseball, the same eye blackened,
Heavy make-up, front tooth out in a jack-o-lantern grin
As she tried to look friendly to the young waitress
Her husband motioned over. He rested one hand
On his wife's shoulder, solicitous, the other waving
A lit cigarette, a small man, dark-haired, now laughing aloud,
Glancing at the uncombed head of his beaten wife again
Turning her back to the room, though not crowded,
All suddenly staring, reading the last few hours
Of those lives in a horror of recognition.
She cupped her hand shading the side of her face,
You could see lumps of vertebrae through her t-shirt,
And he kept on talking, smiling at her, with a slight tilt
Of his head, as if saying *poor baby, something happened to her,*
Good thing I'm here to take care of her, a car wreck,
A bad one, a smash-up, and all of us looked
And knew better. At the table with them was a little girl.
The man, the woman, the five-year-old daughter—
Even the man and the beaten woman had the same features,
As people do who have lived together for years. I couldn't see
The child's face. He was jotting a note on a small pad,
The waitress's name, as if to write a letter praising
Her fine service, and she smiled through her horror, she

Hardly more than sixteen, with clear pale skin. Next to us
A woman in permed hair and suit rose to leave, lunch untouched,
With her daughter. She carried a leather legal-size folder.
We left soon after, heads turned, not looking,
Because sometime the man and woman would go
Home to the privacy of a city apartment, no neighbors
Home all day to hear, but first I said, in the restaurant,
Across the room where he couldn't hear, *If I had a gun*
I'd blow his brains out, and I thought of that moment
Familiar from movies, the round black hole in the forehead
Opening, the back of the skull blowing out frame by frame
Like a baseball smashing a window, but no one near
Would've even been bloodied because no one was standing anywhere
Near him, his hand on the beaten woman's shoulder
Might as well have been yards from his body.

I was taught not to write about this. But my teacher,
A man with a reputation who hoped I would make
Good, never knew that I too have been hit in the face by a man.
He knew only my clumsy efforts to cast what happened
Into "characters," and he loved beauty in poetry.
Maybe what I had written was awkward. Maybe my teacher
Guessed what happened and forbade me writing it
For some good reason, he cared for me, or he feared
He too might've slapped my face, because I, like the character
In that first effort, was bitching to the heavens and a redneck
Boyfriend, and we argued outdoors, near a stack of light wood
Used to kindle the stove like everyone has
In the foothills of North Carolina. That day I railed
Like a caricature of a bitching redneck woman,
Hands on hips, sometimes a clenched fist, I was
Bitching, I think, as he planned some stupid thing
I hated, like fishing, pitching horseshoes, driving
To visit his mother on Sundays, her tiny house

Tangled in dirt roads where she sat in the kitchen dipping snuff.
Whatever he wanted to do was harmless,
But so was my shrieking, my furious pleading, an endless loop
Inside my head rolling *I want to be rid of him*, and he slapped me
Across my open mouth, I felt myself shut up and staggered,
Because he was a large man, and I was a large woman,
He had to make sure he hit me pretty hard,
Both of us strong and mad as hell, early
One Saturday morning, when he wanted to do what he wanted to do
And I wanted to keep him from it. He slapped me
Twice, open-handed, knocking me, open-handed, to my knees
In kindling, so my knees were scraped bloody and my hand
Closed on a foot and a half of inch-thick pine, and I stumbled up
Swinging, my eyes popping wide, till I brought it down
Hard across his shoulder, I saw how the rage on his face
Flashed to fear, just that quick, a second, or less,
And he turned to run but he made the wrong choice,
If he'd gone to the road I wouldn't've followed, but he ran
Inside my "duplex" apartment, an old country house
Cut in two. So I cornered him upstairs and knocked him out.
It was simple. He fell so hard, I thought, I've killed him;
I was throwing my clothes in a paper bag when I heard him
Sobbing. In the bathroom mirror I found the black eye and lop-sided lip,
And it seemed as if I might still take it back, the last ten minutes,
The chase, the beating, the high-pitched screaming,
The stubborn need to go fishing. But the make-up I disdained
In those years—I had just turned twenty—didn't do much
To cover the bruises. His face was clear. The knot on his head
Stopped swelling under ice. It was easy to tell him
To get the hell out and only regret it every other minute
Since there were no children, no marriage, even,
And I was young and believed I had proven
I was strong. I had beaten a man to his knees.
Months later I would go to college and stay safely there for years,

Not letting on to anyone the terrible thing I'd done, until I wrote
That clumsy poem with the unbelievable characters, and now I've tried
To do it again, this time with different characters, I've defied
My teacher, who meant for me to learn to write well,
Who meant for the world to think well of me,
And I am not sorry. If he asked why I would say
I had to do it, and that lie would be like the lie of living
Without telling, till one day seeing the beaten face,
What scared me most, the missing tooth, the tangled hair, the vertebrae,
The daughter. There is no use thinking what it means
About me to say this: I am not sorry. I might have killed
That man. I might have blown his brains out.

TRACY AND JOE

You don't want to know how quiet my life's become
That last night when I heard someone scream *Whore!*
It was one in the morning and I was so bored
With black-and-white sitcoms on the all-night station
I hit the mute button on the remote control,
Sidled to the window, and parted the curtains
Just a slice so no one would see me but I could watch
What was going on and do something about it
If it came to that—call the cops, step outside and hope
My mere presence would settle the fight, if that's what
It was; and it was, all right. Two young men
Pursued a woman, their silhouettes in streetlight,
Her permed hair. Her red sports car was parked
Against the curb. "I'm not lying, Joe!" Her voice
Was shaking. "Don't talk down to me!" Joe was
The tall one, in droopy jeans. "Fucking whore!"
Joe shouted, and the short guy, slight, started
Screaming too: "Pussy! Cunt!" Then my own voice:
"Stop fucking with her!" I didn't care if they heard.
I wanted to fight and get it over with. I saw
The woman run to the car. The men turned back
To the little blue house. I flipped the phone book
To the police station number. I closed it back
And poured a drink of water. One-fifteen. I thought
About sleeping. Then I heard they were at it again.
This time I opened my front door, slowly. I saw
The woman fling her car door wide, jump in
Like an arrow drawn to its target, click on the lights
And peel out into the street. Behind her the men
Stood waving their fists. "Whore! Cunt! Pussy!"
Then they lowered their voices. Tracy, they called her.
Called her "whore" again. "Did you fuck her?"
The tall one, Joe, challenged. "No, man, I wouldn't
Do that to you!" the slim one objected. "Have you
Got a cigarette?" Joe handed one over. "You

Wouldn't fuck her if she spread her legs? Could you
Stop? With her laying right there in front of you?"
The short guy tried to change the subject.
"Come on, let's be friends. What are you
Pissed off about? You got your way." He said it
Bitterly. "Stupid girls! They spread their legs
And you put your dick between them!" The night
Was quiet. Every word was clear. It was easy
To understand what he meant. Women spread
Their legs. Men put their dicks between them.
They think they can't stop. That's how it seems.
Maybe they want the stopping to start before
Anything else does. They don't say so. Maybe they
Think they're doing a favor. Maybe they think
There'll be gratitude later. Maybe they feel sorry
For someone lonely. Maybe they want the sense
Of adventure. Maybe they want to be told they're
Good. Maybe they think they love someone.
I watched the young men. They stopped talking.
I wondered where the woman had fled for comfort.
Today a man parked a car I'd never seen in the drive
Of Joe's little house. He stared out the window,
His forehead glowing. Was he one of them?
I couldn't tell. In the hot afternoon I watched
Through the blinds till my vision wavered. Then
The phone rang, a credit card company, and when
I came back the driveway was empty. I hadn't heard
The engine start or a car door slam. It was quiet
Everywhere, wind sweeping birdsong
Into the empty street. I'm not afraid. But I know
Truth when I hear it. Tracy peeling out
Into the night where now you'd never guess
That drama played here, and I memorized the lines
Like I'd already heard them a thousand times.

For Months She Came At Night, A Strange Presence

like the beating of something flying
against the glass or the swirl of water
in a conch shell, a shadow of a shadow.
Then she got more bold, could unhinge
the porch door silently, help herself
to berries or bread. First I thought I
imagined the hole in the muffins as if
something with a beak found a way in.
And then, the trail of crumbs downstairs
out to the pond. One morning before guava
rose over the skin of water, it was the
second night I couldn't sleep and wanted
at least to see sun rise when I saw some
thing nobody would believe unless they
believed in angels. A woman, mostly a
woman, with wings in the wet grass with
doves and geese. She didn't have arms,
not like a thalidomide baby, but more like
another bird. An angel, except for a huge
beak where the Christmas cards have soft
lips usually smiling. She started to move,
to walk into the water but I beckoned, put
my hand out to her as if nothing seemed
strange and after she hesitated she kind
of fluttered up toward me, her head
lowered as if she was sure I'd be afraid.
That must have been, I realized later, what
she expected of most women. *I'm Leda's
girl* she whispered cowering inside those
wings that were like a screen I imagined
her camouflaged behind, some Gipsy Rose
Lee doing a costume change, coming out
with a basket of fruit on her head. "The
daughter of rape," she hissed, more like

the geese, getting bolder. *My mother was*
ravished, raped. Without arms, I could be
Venus. Without arms, she could have loved
me but these wings remind her of that day
everything changed. Now I crouch like
statues of angels in the gardens rain and
sleet pelt, earthbound and cracked,
still dream of flight

The Gathered Stones

(after the Stoning of Soraya M.)

1

This is what happens: the village boys who are old enough
set out with the canvas sacks
their fathers have strapped to their shoulders
to gather the sharpest stones, the desert morning
lush with marketplace poppies and marigolds
standing in buckets beside the gates of the rich,
the bleating and peaceable shitting of goats on the clovered hills.

2

And this: the accused alone in her mother's room
getting ready as slowly as possible, dressing herself in white,
a white lace scarf to fit under
her chador, which must be black;

it is not lost on her, the irony of how like her wedding this is
while she brushes her silken hair and pinches her last pearl button
through its brocade, and sings a prayer verse
to keep herself well-distracted

3

and the stones go on filling the children's sacks,
first a few rolled over between small fingers, inspected,
found pleasing to God,
then all they can carry, jagged or not, their burdens becoming
too heavy or not…

4

She still could escape: the cypress motions to her
outside the tiny back window, but she has been schooled
in honor, so she calls her daughters in and gives one
her locket, one the ring her grandmother gave her

5
and her tethered camel stares at nothing…

6
The men—her neighbors, the widowed mechanic,
her younger brother, her teenaged sons—are clapping
pairs of stones together in rhythm
like shuffling boots; the jesters her husband has hired for later
are painting their faces;

her father has finished digging the trench
in which will stand her living ankles kneecaps vagina
before the proceedings begin
and remain standing up in the earth
unhurt

long after her back snaps

7
may the doves forever pummel the skies of heaven

as she gathers the gauzy poppies safely into her basket
for the table at home, at evening

8
and no poem comes of this

ODE TO AN EX

It wasn't your body
I chose to bare
Not your knees knocking nude
below my mini-skirt
Or your gold nugget nipples
bragging braless beneath my blouse
Yet you staked your claim
Certain that the dowry
denoted ownership
Title transferred
with marriage certificate
I should have known when you
punched my lab partner in college
for standing too close
That you were the one
standing too close
Squeezing me out
so you could come in
But John Wayne and God
trained me good
to see passion in possession
They don't help me see it now
through swollen black eye memories
Or feel it with a blue bruised heart
Because John Wayne is dead
And God became a girl

Panes

Perhaps she sensed him near: that prickle
that skims the skin like a loosed curl
against a bared neck. Some shivering proof
that we are not so removed from animals:
for our fear also has a throb, a scent. Or
did he speak in low tones, come close
and touch her elbow tentatively
like an old friend disremembered,
his face unfamiliar
until she stepped into the cold
glow of the street lamp along the avenue,

saw the awful truth in his eyes
as he circled away, startled by a beam of light
from a window above where some wife turned down
the narrow bed for her surly husband,
carried a thick blanket to the Davenport
in the dim living room, then lay
down with her ears pressed between pillows,
a cold cloth against her purpling, puffy eye;

where a graying woman awoke behind the shades
of her dream about kids' slaughter and nanny goat screams
on a farm long since plowed under by progress,
turned on the bedside lamp to listen,
then lay back staring at shadows
that spread like bloodstains
on the ceiling, remembering her dead father
and her hatred of his assassin's hands,
his impenetrable, stony heart. Like a feral dog

with a taste of flesh from the injured lamb,
the stranger returned again and again
to cut her off from the flock—and not a stab

of guilt from those above, who heard
or watched, pulled back the heavy curtains
at the first cry, let them fall across the paned
glass squared onto the scene,
ears pressed to the window, cold
with March's sudden chill,
while the vile animal played
out his purpose—no clean kill,
but a torturous game, toying with her as men do

in Friday night bars with lithe smiles
and heavy-lidded eyes. Those weapons
that disarm a girl until she submits
and yields to his rough hands, the hot blade
of his tongue, his rapacious sex, the cold steel
of a morning abandoned. Girls who are the blessed

ones on this spring night: lucky to weep alone, alive
in the dark, to draw down their simple green
window shades, pull up around their bargained bodies
their grandmother's pieced quilts
brought with them from Cincinnati or Albany.
Her deliberate stitches sutured
the squared remnants of outgrown girlhood
dresses, school skirts and blouses,
then the sharp needle nicked the heart-
and-flower pattern, piecing
together those worn-soft memories
of an innocence lost.

ANOTHER VIGIL AT SAN QUENTIN

Not quite midnight. My candle stutters
under the half-full moon, the frightened stars.

Someday in the future, people will be curious
about these rituals; how
we murdered them at dead of night, scientifically,
thinking ourselves modern.

And some of us, the lecturer will explain,
were guards (two rows of them here,
visors pushed back, batons at the ready),
and some were newsmen, clambering over low rooftops
with their klieg lights and cameras,
and the rest of us were weary and defiant,
arm in arm, with our candles and sage

and We Shall Overcome and in this case, eagle feathers,
for the killer is a Native American man
who, drunk, lured a girl-child to his car,
raped, sodomized—go on, tell it—stripped and flung
her broken ten-year-old body from a bridge into a gully,
as if she were a beer can he'd just crushed and left for litter.

Say that part. And then how,
to express our horror
at the ravage of our daughter,
we'll carefully poison him. The candles burn down.
The counter-protesters, Christians to a man,
get on their megaphone. "Ten minutes to repent!
Nine more minutes or your soul will burn!
Eight minutes and the Lord is your judge!"

Our songs pick up as well; We Shall Not
We Shall Not Be Moved,

Gonna Lay Down My Sword and Shield,
and a Navajo chant. The current swells. Inside,
a frightened, fucked-up man
is being prepared for death and burial.
He has requested that a medicine man, with sage,
accompany him in his death chamber. Request denied.
All right, one eagle feather,

to be pinned to the sheet over his body.

I link arms with the rough wool coat next to me,
bow my head into a friend's shoulder,
thinking about my own rape
at the hands of a raging drunk, years ago.

I don't have words
for what I'm doing here, only the smell
of the ocean, going on and on below us:
crash, smash, gotcha,
and the softness of air on my cheeks,
and the gulls screaming.
Last week the rains finally stopped.
The peach tree is in full pink flower.
Earth seems to have forgiven
our uncountable human sins again
and opened her arms to us again in spring. Oh pure

Right and Wrong, how I long for you!
Tell the people of the future
I came here for confusion,
and ignorance, and darkness.
For the orange lick of flame against the char of ash,
for poison and reason, and the old moon,
and a stubborn idea about innocence.

A GRAPPLE OF SPARROWS

For Lara Logan

On the sidewalk, a tumbleweed
of feathers nip and grip one another,
a silent grapple of sparrows.

Soon obvious which one's male,
he pins the twist of her to the ground,
bites her neck until she holds still,

before the kerfuffle of wings begins again.
They skitter across the concrete,
fall off the curb to land under a car.

A woman asks, *Are they fighting
or mating? Not much difference to her
either way,* I reply. I keep watching

for five minutes, maybe ten, the longest
I've stopped for a New York street show
in years. A girl asks her mom

what the birds are doing, and she says,
*It's spring, honey, they're doing
what birds do in spring.*

Still, the mating looks like fighting to me,
the female's head torqued, her bulging eyes
and gaped beak, the male's claws around her

like rope, his beak wielded like a knife,
his wings a thump-tick of lust, the slight
weight of him enough to hold her down.

ANGLERFISH

For Iman al-Obeidi

What if we women were anglerfish, our lures
springing from our foreheads, an irresistible
lighthouse of hunger, our giant-toothed jaws
so unhinged we could swallow prey twice our size?
What if our men were small, unable to feed
on their own, equipped with little more
than a powerful nose with which to find us,
starving to death if they don't? When they find us
and bite into our sides, what if they were
to dissolve like angler males, becoming
an ever-ready portable sperm factory
hanging off us, of which we might carry six?
No more forest of barstools to hack through
on a Friday night, hoping to meet a kind
baboon in a clearing. No more detention
at the checkpoint for no good reason, no more
booze poured in our eyes, nose, mouth, vagina,
no more army boots to the head, no more
gun-barrel rapes, no more running naked
down the street begging for help from people
who blame us for our blood-streaked thighs.

To Judge Faolain, Dead Long Enough: A Summons

Your Honor, when my mother stood
before you, with her routine
domestic plea, after weeks
of waiting for speech to return
to her body, with her homemade
forties hairdo, her face purple still
under pancake, her jaw off just a little,
her *holy of holies* healing,
her breasts wrung, her heart
the bursting heart of someone
snagged among rocks deep
in a sharkpool – no, not "someone,"

but a woman there, snagged
with her babies, *by* them,
in one of hope's pedestrian,
brutal turns – when, in the tones
of parlors overlooking the harbor,
you admonished that, for the sake
of the family, the wife
must take the husband back to her bed,
what you will not to see before you
was a women risen clean to the surface,
a woman who, with one arm flailing,
held up with the other her actual
burdens of flesh. When you clamped
to her leg the chain of *justice*,
you ferried us back down to *the law*,
the black ice eye, the maw, the mako
that circles the kitchen table nightly.
What did you make of the words
she told you, not to have heard her,
not to have seen here there? Almost-
forgivable ignorance, you were not

the fist, the boot, or the blade,
but the jaded, corrective ear and eye
at the limits of her world. Now

I will you to see her as she was, to ride
your own words back into light. I call
your spirit home again, divesting you
of robe and bench, the fine white hand
and half-lit Irish eye. Tonight, put on
a body in the trailer down the road
where your father, when he can't
get it up, makes love to your mother
with a rifle. Let your name be
Eva-Mary. Let your hour of birth
be dawn. Let your life be long
and common, and your flesh endure.

GRATEFUL

·   I

In the village, when the news broke

-- of the two sixth-grade girls, ambushed
in the woods on their way home from school,
raped, tortured, the one surviving
staggering naked onto the tracks so bloody
the trainmen thought the head-to-toe red
was a garment –
    a local friend, by way of
explanation, spilled a couple of local wisecracks:
*What makes a woman beautiful? he said. Jelly doughnuts
and incest.* The boys had been named

who'd dragged the mattresses to the woods,
the guns, the dirty magazines, the axes,
and waited. The whole town knew those boys.
The whole town knew the families
in which those boys were learning this was
sex, the one, in which – the whole town
knew – the son practiced on his sister,

With his Dad. And that silent
little girl? I know what she thought, day,
night: another thing to get used to,
growing up.

·   II

Once, as a child, in an iron lung of dread
the long years of your absence, I told
the priest in confession, the priest Father Welch,
who came to watch the Sox and drink ice tea.
He told me to mind my father.

To obey.

So I put my soul to bed by itself,
so far away that as a woman I still can't
find it. And waited to grow up, to be
a person in the Great World, where men
would be as safe to know as dogs. But, brother,

each line and verse I learned augmented
those seeds of dread, to one Great Wood,
to interlocking branches. Though I often
prayed for you to come home and save me,

looking back I'm grateful
from what kept you away from *the game the whole family*
can play. Robed, studying to be
a priest, you were learning, in books illumined
in gold, the statutes of the overarching code: what

in other words, we both were spared
your learning at our father's knee, on me.

Two Teachers Leaving

A colleague told me
a student cut her wrist in class today,
raged on herself over a boyfriend cheating.
Teacher did not see it happen,
only the blood break
through the seams of her hand
when another student yelled *look!*
Police dismissed the class to the hall,
rubber-gloved paramedics
cleaned stains from the floor,
a counselor consoled only the victim.

I wanted to share my pain that same day
the fractured mind of one of my students enflamed
when her partner stole the drugs they bought together,
left a swollen cut on her lip.
Student shouted *I hate her*
just after I accepted her late paper.
Throw your F-ing smile out the F-ing window!
You're scared of me she shouted.
Struggling there in a poison,
twenty-nine students stopped awkwardly.
I recalled her mother saying,
send her to the hall when she gets vicious.

When adolescence empties a magazine of verbal violence
upon the nearest human being,
it feels like a bullet in a drive-by.
Two teachers leaving like this
ought to have affirmed one another.
Instead we carried the assault
and limped off in opposite directions.
I recall the scent of linen in my car,

a brief silence interrupted by the sound
of ignitions firing up one after another.
A grey sky slit its throat
in our rear-view mirrors.

A Grecian Ode

The guy who approached me
on the steps of the Athens museum
said *nothing inside*

is as beautiful as you.
Before we used "trafficking"
as the prime-time euphemism

for the sex slave trade,
he promised me a camera,
one like Ansel Adams used.

But I knew he would be disappointed;
because I was, on close inspection,
artless, clumsy, monkey-minded

definitely more asymmetric
than anything on an urn. So,
not wishing to disappoint him,

I said no.
If he had asked me
to help him find his puppy,

today I'd probably be a toothless discard
from some hellhole
in Thessalonika.

Even now my flaws
make me comfortable in their home;
Father and Mother me.

Gautier D'Agoty's Écorchés

Anatomie des parties de la génération, Paris, 1773

What have they done to deserve this beauty?
Did they, like Marsyas, invite some knife-
wielding God with petty transgressions,
the crime of a few tunes on Athena's lost flute?

Or were they simply too poor for deep
graves, locked gates, and good husbands
to watch over the mounds of new soil
tossed toward them and their hunted unborn?

Whoever they were, they're still with us,
posing demurely in suits of blood
and muscle, the bruised shadows
of what skin they do have, purpling like

crushed petunias as they spread their legs
and raise their meaty arms to show
dissected breasts, unfinished infants, sundry
viscera on the ground about their feet

as if this were Thanksgiving and they
cornucopias stuffed with squash and fruit.
And who delivered their sentences?
Surely not the muses who, at least,

let them keep rococo faces. In 1773
the womb and brain were the last outposts
of the body to be mapped. D'Agoty bought
the rights to Le Blon's technique of printing

mezzotints and gave these ladies homes
in scientific texts, but anatomists believed
D'Agoty's prints too gorgeous to be accurate.
Perhaps that's why they open other wounds

so easily in us. All so like the single rabbit
I downed at twenty with a borrowed rifle,
and then was obligated to see skinned,
first scoring the length of the spine,

then peeling the fur in one steaming piece,
while the perverse uncle who clearly desired
to touch me, instead held up a dripping pelt
in one hand, and in the other, a flayed carcass

still wrapped in its bundle of muscle like a gift.

ROUGH MUSIC, *EDINBURGH 1829*

Why shouldn't Dr. Knox have invited
his painter friend to view the body
of the girl he knew was too fresh
for legitimate death, her "handsome"
limbs and alabaster waist a crime
to cut before at least one brush
could render her unscathed on paper?
Had she been any less an odalisque,
perhaps he wouldn't have needed to collude
with artists or waste good whiskey
to keep the cream in her hips, her purpled
lips all the more arresting than they'd been
in life. If he'd found her sooner and living
would he have known all this was there
for purchase? Would he have offered
to keep her in dresses and tea for peeks?
In the weeks after Hare had turned
King's evidence on Burke and the latter's
convicted corpse was flayed and offered up
to forty thousand pairs of public eyes,
Knox refused to speak. Though by report
she'd been delivered to Surgeons Square
still warm and clutching twopence-halfpenny
someone paid to bed her, they cut her hair
before she cooled, and Mary swam three
months in whiskey before they took her skin
apart to look inside. When the story broke,
an angry mob came after Knox with noise,
an opera of whistles, pots and pans,
and tore his effigy to shreds in Newington
outside his house. And if in Mary Paterson
a child had taken root, no one would be the wiser
if Knox had kept the little lyric of it to himself,

scion fathered by the Scottish city's lust,
gift to men of science, and so also to me,
woman of the new world digging through
old books to resurrect her murdered parts,
to offer her my own rough music, the strange
collusion of imaginary science and real art.

Tongue

The problem is not night—people gathering in booths—or a game
where you select who to save from an apartment that's on fire.

But at night, the silver bathroom stalls in the Multiplex crack open
as if I am the last horse to wander out during the credits.

What I mean is, my thighs sometimes still feel like the whites of a poached egg.
There is logic to thinking about digger wasps, solitary insects that excavate

nests from the soil and then straddle their prey, usually an August cricket,
ashy as the blade of a waterlogged feather. And at night, the hermit thrush

calls, flutters to a new tree, calls, and soon the grove hosts a quorum
of these nightingale songs when there is only one traveling from tree to tree,

to an oak like the one shading my porch—I go there at night to breathe.
In the myth of Philomela, the King puts his knife down Philomela's throat

after he finishes, then cuts her tongue out. Before she becomes a thrush,
she weaves what happened: images in a bolt of cloth, a kind of flag.

The newspaper pays for them, the flickering paper flags
leaning on the bottom panel of the doors in the neighborhoods.

Again this year, before dawn, the truck door slammed—I heard
someone cross the street. When I woke, flames were mouthing the air.

Oral History

You missed out on Benny.
You weren't born yet.
He was one of Mom's real winners,
Mexican guy, a gang member
with tattoos and a big knife.
He used to grab Jamie
by the hair,
throw him
across the room.

My job was to catch
the poor kid
before he hit
the wall.

My sister tells me this
from her hospital bed
fifty-odd years later,
recovering from another surgery
related to her Vicodin
abuse. Our mother's ashes rest
a few miles away in a small crypt
at Inglewood, near
the tiny box
containing our other sister,
the one who didn't
make it out. Hundreds of miles
to our north, Jamie heads
downtown for his daily dose
at the Methadone clinic.

Did you know,
I ask my sister, that brain injuries –
actual holes in the brain –
can be caused purely by
emotional trauma?

Eighty-nine pounds
of survival, she looks
at me with our mother's
huge blue eyes.

No shit,
she says.

THE RIVER IS THE SEA

Whenever I walk along a city's river at night,
I am reminded of a man whose name I never knew.
I remember his face, a sharp, shadowed thing,
not because I desired him, or because the moon
shone on the river in a way I'll never forget—
I did forget it—but because this man desired me
with violence and ugliness. I was in a European city
for the first time, but I had spent my life
walking along flowing water. The creek
behind my childhood home marked my kingdom,
and though I waded to my knees, played
with pieces of trash, and crossed the gully
on fallen trees, I never broke a bone or bled.
But the man by the river in that city pushed me
against the railing, shoved his hand beneath my shirt,
and would not let me go. For three seconds. Statues
on the nearby bridge looked in other directions,
and somehow, no people passed. Those seconds
were a lifetime, or, I thought, the end of mine.
I said no in every language I knew.
He was small, but so strong that when I moved,
I did not move. I didn't know when I screamed
he'd let me go. Never underestimate the music
of a woman's scream: the sound the river would make
if it did not wish to go to the sea, if every current
resisted and turned around. Running back to my room
down the cobble-stoned street, I promised
to get to where I wanted to go, to what the girl
dangling her feet above the creek dreamed of.
The river does want to go to the sea
because the river is the sea. Rushing past buildings
that late hour, and even now, I am the river:
a gathering of water made beautiful,
not by the moon, but by how I will not stop.

AUBADE

After he leaves she waits
on her side of the bed each night
makes her way 'round its length and breadth
slides carefully by the opened windows
around sharp corners
of the hard oak frame
to get to the other side.

Weeks pass.
She realizes she can be more
centered toward the middle.
By the seventh week she packs her books
moves them to his side table
sleeps on the right first time in six years.

Comfortable there she embraces the distance
leaves the shades open
eyes and ears touching the leaves.

No more maneuvering the bed's path
or fear of falling out of the third story window.
Morning light enters
more easily now.

SLIDING DOWN

A white-bearded cook
putting broccoli stems in my waitress apron,
and random slaps to my teenage ass.
After work a walk to Dave's old house

with Miri, Scott, and Chaim.
A finished bottle of bourbon,
me sliding down and out my chair
and under the table in the abandoned duplex.

Scott walks me home, his arm under me
for support, showing me how to smoke a cigarette
in the rain, opening beer caps with his mouth.
We detour through the park,

put our hands into each other's shirts,
touching new skin.
He's kissing me with his eyes closed, I try to close mine too,
but I'm in an elevator falling from the top floor,

too drunk for him and this.
I start to walk away from his hard cock—
you're a tease, he follows.
I say: *I can give you a hand job that's it, I'm too drunk.*

I don't want a hand job.
He starts kissing me again, violent, fast, sloppy.
I keep my mouth closed and he hates that.
He grabs my upper arm and swings me hard down to the ground.

My bare back on asphalt scraped and red,
head banging against chain link fence.
A borrowed stretched out pink tank-top,
missing undies and broken zipper

khaki pants in the trash.

The Nightmare's Hand

Still swimming in night-milk
you watch like a movie
the lived dreams of your childhood
and grandma
putting out plates of food in her kitchen

The memory of that soft-edged blackness
steals furry in your brain
You can see it
on the inside
of your skull bone
on the private side
of your forehead
the soft black cloud
like the deadly creep
of a flameless fire
that seductively kills

There's a rocking of the bed
and under the elastic of your striped pajamas
a hand creeps
You remember the finest of black hairs
          on the knuckles

That's why the animals crouch in burrows
in the small hollows of your mind
awake in the night

That's why they huddle there
in the darkened hole of memory
until light cracks
Then, only then
do they creep from their small, secret holes
to find the knots of green to eat
and you the faces of yellow eggs
and the coughing sharpness of toast

The Boys, the Broom Handle, the Retarded Girl

Who was asking for it—
Everyone can see
Even today in the formal courtroom,
Beneath the coarse flag draped
Across the wall like something on a stage,
Which reminds her of the agony of school
But also of a dress they let her wear
To a parade one time,
Anyone can tell
She's asking, she's pleading
For it, as we all
Plead—
Chews on a wisp of hair,
Holds down the knee
That tries to creep under her chin,
Picks at a flake of skin, anxious
And eager to please this scowling man
And the rest of them, if she only can—
Replies *I cared for them, they were my friends*

It is she of whom these boys
Said, afterward, *Wow, what a sicko*,
It is she of whom they boasted
As we all boast

Now and again, because we need,
Don't we, to feel
Worthwhile—
As without thinking we might touch for luck
That flag they've hung there, though we'd all avoid
Touching the girl.

AFTER HE BREAKS HER ARM

there's little I can do—the small conveyance
from the porch where she sat, one busted tooth
in her hand, to the hospital where she says,

car accident, just me, please, no cops.
In the harbor of my house, she sleeps
in my bed, the angles of her body wrapped

in my oversized pajamas, one sleeve
cut off for the cast. I wake her with tea,
burnt toast, runny eggs, though she winces

when she chews, the black whorl on her jaw
now haloed in green. Until her right eye
opens, I read her books, whatever's handy,

whatever keeps her here. Once, to cheer her,
I paint her nails, each a different color,
the enamel smearing up to her knuckles

when the crying starts again. The eighth night,
when she tells me she misses him, I'm kneeling
in the bethel of the bathroom, bent over

the tub, raking a razor through the thick
lather on her legs, and when she says,
take me home, I nick her ankle just enough

to draw blood, one rusty drop that slides
to the surface of the water, shimmies
its tendrils into the murk, and is gone.

MUM

1. **mum** (interj.) 1568, from M.E. *mum, mom* "silent" (1377), imitative of the sound made with closed lips, as indicative of unwillingness or inability to speak.

> As in, *When it came to talking about what happened to her*
> *in that boy's house when she was twelve, she was mum.*

It's not like it doesn't happen all the time.

It happens to old ladies. It happens to little
girls. When it is done by a group the shame
is multiplied.

So when, over the top of a car, after the two
of us opened up our doors, ready to enter,
my cousin announced that it happened to
my mother, too, she said it as though
I already knew.

Mothers do keep things from their daughters.

If only I had known I would have known
to be afraid of even the friendliest of strangers.

2. **mum** (n.1) abbreviation of *chrysanthemum*, first attested 1924 in the jargon of gardeners. Chrysanthemums: Any of a genus of plants related to the daisies including some grown for their showy bloom or for medicinal products or insecticides.

> As in, *On her walk with those boys, before they got to that house,*
> *she picked a handful of golden mums.*

So many varieties of Asteraceae (Compositae).
Some perennials, some annuals.
According to Sunset West Gardeners, they thrive
   in "All Zones, Except as Noted";
   all require "Regular Water, Except as Noted."

Arctic is a hardy perennial; self-sufficient, accustomed to hardship.
Costmary is frugal, weedy. Dusty Miller & Silver Lace, finely cut.

Feverfew's aggressive, compact. Gold & Silver are always on call,
prohibited in areas. Marguerite & Paris are short lived Norma Jeans.
Ox-Eye & Common are resourceful, if not pretty. Shasta is leathery.
Summer sports cleavage; a coquette. Florist's is the most useful,
versatile, valued for its varied forms:

> Anemone loves water; Brush loves comb;
> Decorative loves sequins; Incurve loves bone;
> Irregular loves braces; Laciniated loves edge;
> Pompom loves pep; Quill, love's ledge; Reflex
> returns; Semidouble, her twin; Daisy loves
> solitude; Spider loves spin; Spoon loves the
> hungry, feeds everyone but herself; in her pantry,
> she is on the shelf.

> My mother is an Arctic Spoon.
> Hardy, and generous. I wish I were a spoon.
> But I am a quill. I am on the ledge.

3. **mum** (n.2) 1823, pet word for "mother," short for mummy. In British
sociology, used from 1957 in ref. to "the working class mother as an influence of
the lives of her children."

> As in, *The girl's mum was always a factory worker: sporting goods, and then
> doorknobs, locks, now flashlights, running efficient machines, hoisting crates of
> anodized steel heads onto a conveyer, catching finished lights as they roll out.*

> It was almost a normal day, a day like most others, a day
> of work that took us halfway around the clock from six 'til
> six. We were working together at the plant. She had put
> in a good word for me and they had given me a job in
> packaging. It must have been spring because I
> remember the sun through the kitchen window after
> returning home.

> It was her home, and she was warming me a cup of
> coffee from the pot she made that morning before we left

for work. We were two grown women, at least I thought of myself as grown, but really, even now, more than a decade later, I still feel small. But I am stalling. I am good at stalling. Right now, I should be putting on paper what was so hard for my mother to find words for.

Mother, verb meaning "to take care of," first recorded 1863.

As in, *Her mother's mothering was often guided by instinctive gestures.*

One evening, when I was about twelve, as I listened to the bside of "Let's Go Crazy", my mother flung open my door, swiped the record from my stereo...

You can funk until the dawn / making love 'til cherry's gone

You can't listen to that! She bends
but it does not break, and, taking a
steak knife, etches deep zig-zags
into the circle of an erotic city I
didn't understand.

The week before, without her
knowledge, I had defied her,
ridden my bike from the B of A
parking lot to the house of a boy,
who, on his bedroom floor, taught
me wrestling techniques.

Mother Tongue, "one's native language," first attested c. 1380.

As in, *Even in her mother tongue, she could find
no words for what happened.*

What other contexts are there for a mother tongue? Sensual, rather than linguistic: licking drips of melted ice cream from the side of a mushy sugar cone; moistening the flap of an envelope; wetting her fingers to wipe dirt from her child's cheek; sucking ketchup from her child's dirty finger; working loose threads of pot roast from between two teeth; flickering over the slippery head of a penis; Oh, the places mother's tongue has been.

1960: *Do it Do it Do it,* the boys chant. Her mother is twelve years old, in a dark room, in a strange house.

1978: *Let's do it,* the boy says, as he leads me to the bathroom at recess. There, in the dirty stall, we pulled our pants down, bumped seven-year-old genitalia together. I remember making my mother promise not to tell Dad.

1985: *Come on, let me do it,* the guy says, yanking his zipper down. *I can't, I can't,* I say, wrenching away, pulling up my pants.

1991: I remember a story a man told me while he was doing *it* to me, holding me hard, after the party had ended: how he came home from work one night, noticed through an open window a girl passed out on his bed, his roommates doing *it* to her; she was unconscious. He rushed in yelling, *Hey! Let me do it to her, too.* When she awoke she was screaming Stop! He just said *I never pass up an opportunity to get laid.*

1993: In my room in the dark I think about *it* every night, wondering if *it* would have ever happened to me had my mother told me *it* had happened to her first.

COLLISION

I get out to look for damage. To run my palms
along the body. To finger the scratches

and newest nicks. The man who hit me
is shaking. I watch him and think

how just this morning over the fence
my neighbor told me her dream:

my children were out on the lawn
frantic and cold; my husband emerged

from the house where windows were gone, curtains
spilling over the sills and I, inside,

had been killed. Before that (oh typical day)
I'd been out walking the dog

when in the rustling pine a rabbit hopped
with an arrow, no wayward thing,

plunged through its skull, exiting its jaw.
How is it this rabbit? This arrow?

How some archer boy on the block let this go.
Same boy I knew summers long ago

who stuffed fireworks into frogs and lit them
on the pier. Who captured cats in pillowcases

and tossed them into traffic. Traffic reeling
past me fixed in the center lane

wondering, now, why the boy
would not bring a shovel to the head.

Discourse

Well, did you… breaks a room
into parts, a diorama.
Flat, well-placed
things. Calculated spaces.
From above, just slits
of paper. I'm in a frame.
I am held still
by my own stiffness. I have
no depth. A cardboard cutout.
This framed-self moves back
and forth from shelf to box
to display case to box
to the dump.
My cardboard self is nicked
and worn. *Well, did you…* ?
Someone throws trash
on the diorama. *Did you*

say something? Spoiled food stuffs
seep into the cardboard. *Did you*

do something? Grunge and wrappers.
Well, did you

suggest something? Loose bits crush
the frame, the scene, the cardboard-
thin me. It is all   called trash now.

HIGH-WATER MARK

I.

Under the ocean, the mountain ranges. The same mutated earthen spines that line up, around us now, are under there. Way under. The longest is 40,000 miles. Below, a timeless body stretches. Between ocean mountain ranges: valleys and an abyss with 90% of earth's living organisms. Pressure in the deepest regions: 8 tons per square inch. A massive pressure of a sunken world. The weight of it all. Pressure to pull the body inwards. All my spaces collapsing.

A skin like a soggy, plastic bag.

II.

A therapist rephrases it as *your assault,* and I settle back into that tough nut of my stomach. I secure the word again in me: Assault. Assault. Not *Rape*. Shhh.

But edges wear. Talk, the ebb and flow, the surviving, the same dark places that wake us. Lines soften. Boxes fade.

Rape, a violence. A taking. A greed. Person made meat and holes. So that assault is no longer the sibling of rape but a conjoined twin. Separate heads and separate torsos housing semi-functioning organs but always the same swollen genitals.

The same kicking legs.

III.
Cunnus and Lingua
Mouth, lips and tongue
Mouth and the breath that moves through it
Lips and the vibrations from stories, sentiments, love songs told through them.
The tongue with yet another language, this one fluent—heavy
or lilting, festive
or sacred.

Mouth, lips and tongue. This does not include your teeth. Their lashing, their tantrum. Your lips, a monster-flesh, stretched around a black hole, demonspeak. A tongue forked, spitting, and stinging. Those rows of teeth. They sink into folds of skin. The work of sharks. The work of blades, of forks. All the things to cut for the chewing.

It is called, after all, *eating out.*

IV.

You tell me I am overreacting. And then you turn like a halibut. Like a flatfish that begins life looking like most salmon. During development, a halibut changes physically to adapt to a bottom-dwelling lifestyle. The body turns sideways and the mouth twists. One eye migrates from one side of the face to the other. You see this way. Looking above. All the time. Belly whitening—a disguise for creatures below—you look like light coming from the surface. The side of you, halibut, skims the ocean floor, sees nothing below. But always eating. A bottom feeder, evolved to be so.

V.

To fog away, drift through a room. To smile a smile that means a smile, nothing more. I am always in danger of being read: the slope of my bangs, a slight to the rest of my forehead. And the way I move my nervous hands from counter top to lap to counter top to lap before finally resting them across my chest. Locked. To some, read like a speck on a lens. A tarnish of the late morning's efforts to hold back the day. Read like the tip of an iceberg to others, great blue-white chills of me under the surface of any word. And often I read like a report of myself. I learned early on to lock my eyes into a particular color, a particular style of rings and spokes. When people look into my eyes and say, *what happened to you was wrong*, I think, *These are my eyes. You are just seeing my eyes.*

VI.

It is only made of teeth and those teeth are only made to bite, they fit exactly into your skin. You thought your skin was solid, you thought you were solid too. But when you look closely, you see there were bite marks before the teeth came. You were made to be pierced, to bleed. Teeth are doing what teeth do. Teeth find you, it's not a surprise, not unwarranted. You are a blueprint. And here, you thought you were the building. Tsk.

VII.

He is a solid tight thing A knot Something has pulled him taut there is no room I try to wiggle free there is no room My friend pulls my arm hard behind my back pushes my face down again I barely feel myself anymore My solid tight friend my knot he says Don't you ever think you aren't sexy. You're beautiful.

VIII.

What is the word. You are reminded of something awful. But it—only lightly, hits the heart and mostly tingles ears. Stretches in tidal pulls across the skin. Does not shake, crack the ribcage to release squawking birds. There is a flinch—a minnow. Escapes. Catch it? Mention it to therapists or friends or a diary? It's not so important. You take note because that is what you do now—take notes and maybe you are only made up of notes that manage this Self. Your new function: to pour over them at 4:12 a.m. Are you now, in fact, actually *okay*?

MOSTLY TO UNCOVER THE REALITY OF MY SOOTHING BRAND OF SICKNESS

I called a dangerous man my husband and something inside me
loved it, loved the way each day he killed me a little more, killed
himself a little more. There were ways of believing everything he
said. Sometimes it meant folding my thoughts into tight squares
with sharp edges that nicked my tongue as I held them underneath.
Sometimes it meant hiding parts of myself in pissy alleyways and
abandoned parking lots where they got slept on and rained on,
pushed around in shopping carts or made a doorway on some tired
body's flimsy house, so that I ended up a vagina with half a heart
and no deep breaths. He never wanted or missed me but he wanted
to, his brutal attachment burning the inside of me like an etching,
toxic and harsh in its carefully planned beauty. I almost believed
I could take it. One day I thought I couldn't fight anymore and then
a sudden shift: I hustled a latticework of craving between blows.
I unlocked my chorus of archetypal women from their chains. They
rubbed their raw wrists with aloe and set to work.

MOTORHOME AGON

for Julie Reiser

It must sound like something is trying
to be born. At home, they were too far
from their neighbors for anyone to hear.

Their house was like the fossil of an egg.

But their walls are thinner now,
so they're throwing things. They are
like insects trapped together under a glass.

She takes their daughter out into the desert.

The girl will remember petrified wood.
Agate rings flowed from her hands
like ripples across the surface of water.

She'll think of the argument years later
while watching a play by Euripides.

The set is sheet metal loosely sewn
together like hides: ringing skins
that thunder like the walls of a motorhome.

Flint spearheads shatter against bronze
as Diana Rigg pounds home her lines as Medea.

Jason only taps in rebuttal.

A band of light slips across the stage
to signify a day.

*

But why a day?

As if any tangle of habits and Fatal threads
could be twisted smooth between
the thumb and forefinger of earth and sun.

In the calendar of shadows on the desert,
it's been twenty-five years.
The woman and her daughter walked

until they found the woman couldn't
take off her ring.

The daughter, who has walked out after
another argument, realizes
the ripples might have been returning.

Reversal and recognition:
catharsis comes with the discovery,
There, but for the grace of God . . .

She keeps walking toward the vanishing point.

*

As the others go by, she wonders
at what cost they maintain the illusion—

if it shields them from what thunders,
if they fear the lack of comfort,
or if they have been exiled from Colchis, Corinth,

or Los Angeles with two young sons.

In a parking lot, she listens
for the sound inside, and wonders if
what would be born will ever,

with its own strength,

break from shadows and translucence
to fill its lungs
with the sharp and oxidizing air

where the deer outside her tent sound like soft rain.

Women and Poetry

They want to be told what's what by a man,
women at the north end of the table nodding together,
one so newly married she writes as if
her poem is her writing hand, lonely for the ring.

I want to be told what's lovely by a man
as I was by my famous teacher who taught women,
especially the beauty seated on his right, to incite riot.
Her pain seemed an Ars Poetica,
her poems all naked body, enticingly sensual,
flushed in sun and shower, come from the pool in stanza one
to become in stanza two an erect and threatening penis
in a changing room shared by a man and a girl.
Was she the child? we wondered. What difference to the poem?

In this class, we sit together in a darkening room, late afternoon.
I am trying to love poetry as a stay against confusion,
flesh for now a stay against death, as lightning, incipient storm,
with its causal gods, breaks closer to morning.

I write alone in the kitchen now with only that growl to push me.
No man's voice here, no transformation, only poetry.

SQUIRREL

On long line at the video store, my weekend
under my arm—*Wait Until Dark, The Glass Menagerie*–
I want to hit him, want to throw her
into my car and drive her to piano or ballet,
where she might give her breasts a chance
to set in their mold, give the bone in her knees
a chance to fuse before the tugging at her soft
joints and sockets begins, the loosening.

Fourteen, tops, she's the kind of pretty
they paste false lashes on and falsies,
splash over the cover of *Cosmo*,
the kind of creamy-pretty men love to spoil.

She's leaning over the counter
where she almost works,
nodding yes to the much older boy,
man, really, old enough to have tattoos,
to have fathered listless children,
who's fidgeting in his Levis
like a corn worm tunneling in its damp husk.

Then she's on the phone to her mother, saying
something about a movie, some other girls, someone's
older sister driving,
safe as a ragdoll and the story floats.

A heat-driven dog off his leash,
he looks like he could spontaneously
combust, he's so excited, like I could just
stand here behind him and blow gently,
coax him into totem-sized flames,
but I walk next-door to the Winn Dixie
for popcorn, cat food.

When I was fourteen, the kind of close,
angular pretty that casts sullen shadows,
the squirrels on Jekyll Island crept out of the trees
to nibble M&Ms from our anxious hands,
and one, hungry and tentative, followed us
into the condo and panicked, flew
circus circles around the room, bounding
wall-to-wall until it smashed into the glass door
and slid dead as wonder to the floor, a slight,
undone softness we buried in a box.

The same day, my father's friend
pulled me by my ankles
to the bottom of the pool as if the plug
had been pulled, the water sucking me down,
and pressed his hand between my legs,
where my uncle had touched, years before
I'd begun to grow this new softer body, the great
effort and absolution of it,

and I pushed against him and the side of the pool
until, finally, I reached air,
though it had changed, the air, into something thin
and ragged, like something you'd keep in a shoebox,
so the way I breathe changed forever.

Outside, the boy's candy blue Nova idles,
a trophy mounted to the parking lot,
a vinyl-sluiced altar to *Sooner*.
A pack of his friends
lean sentry on the hood, smoking
like it takes a great talent,
the filling and emptying of their lungs,
like it's something they deserve.

He nudges her in,
eases with feral concentration
into the seat beside her, slams the door,
and it feels as if he's dragged
all the air in with him, the rare, damaged air,
leaving nothing between us but glass.

KITCHEN TABLE REFUGE

kitchen table refuge particle board circle became my roof my little home a
center in the dysfunction the flying glass above me the hard words that even
though i was three and could read i wouldn't dare use hiding from the booze
and fists and feet that my grandfather never aimed at me but that hit home
anyway hiding from the future when he would aim something more dangerous that my grandma blocked but that hit home anyway my imaginary friends
breadcrumbs that i talked to all with names starting with v . . . veronica
victoria vivian vanessa almost driving him crazy in his delirium tremors his
withdrawal making him think i'd already lost what mind i had the alcohol
filled cough elixir i spooned down him as he was "sick" trying to make him
feel better trying to take away the pain i was sane enough to hide from circle
of false wood assimilated trees reconstituted reality you absorbed the shock of
tears of kicks of stories of time and death and i hauled you two thousand miles
after my grandma passed scarred with scratches with burns from cigarettes and
hot spoons my uncle dropped in a cloud of black tar i can't let go of you anymore than i can let go of the good food and bad memories the family recipes i
change to suit my needs those of my children none of whom have names starting with v anymore than i can let go of the taste of laughter mixed with tears

Camera Obscura

She dreams of crushing *Viagra*
into dust and hurling it into oceans.
If whales became sudden Casanovas
beating their lusty tails and breeching up a frenzy
it won't bother her. Whales are not men.

Out of the corner of her eye, she sees herself
rocking and rolling with the man who rode her to hell.
She shouldn't have to see that. Better to look
through kinder apertures—the church, or the psychiatrist.
Sometimes, regally, with the conviction of a feminist,
she rides the light as if it were a stallion—
sits astride it, breathless, subordinating it to her will.
Like David Copperfield (the illusionist not the child
of the illusionist) she makes the laws of physics
as compliant as an old celery stalk.
She can do this because she's a woman over fifty.

But then, alas, the summer ends and pinholes start to prick.
The sour tongue revives its familiar, dull invasion,
digging out the fillings in her molars, loosening the bridge
the orthodontist (a kind man but a man nevertheless)
inserted with tenderness to rectify her smile. By now
she has been realigned and resurrected just about
as much as she can stand. She is bored to death.
So today, twenty-eight years after the attack,
a team of male detectives will try to figure out why
she did it when they find her naked on the chessboard vinyl
floor of her master bathroom, her eyes suffused with joy.

Balanced on a ledge as thin as a razorblade just above
the bald detective's head she'll witness their clumsy
game of clues. She won't give a damn when they don't get it right
because, in this new place (where time is light-made-manifest),
she can already see that vile stump of a word with pinhole clarity—
           Rape!....Rape!....Rape!
dancing itself to death on the folds of her own magnificent wings.

TAKE BACK THE NIGHT

We don't speak of why we're here,
if it happened to us, or not,
or if it was a friend. The statistics
say there is one in four. We pass
each other markers, call each other *sister*

walking past fraternity row, the boys
pouring out from their porches to stare
beers in hand, leering at the thread
of women, *stupid bitches, dykes.*
It's dark and I try to look at their faces,

remembering my friend Andrea, weeks earlier
telling me about being gang raped at the Delta
Chi house, how they took turns, making her swallow,
then chug a beer, until they left her in a pool
of her own blood and puke and

we're chanting *Women Unite! Take Back
the Night*, my voice rising up meeting
the others. I wonder if our voices reach them, if this
makes their stomachs turn, if years later,
when they touch another woman,

will they remember her? I don't remember
how she got home, how any of us will,
but we do. We walk in pairs, glancing
over our shoulders. Our hearts pounding
out the chant, our silent rhythm played

over again down Lake Street, down the
winding path of our lives, as we gather distance
from that point. How clear the sky was that April,
when we let our voices loose,
the sky shattering, with stars.

SMALL MIRACLES

Give me strength this day, O Lord God of Israel! (Judith 13,6-8)

The menorah waxy from last year's
miracles, I take the butter knife
from the drawer and begin the ritual
scraping away of that which has hardened
and remained.

My friend Lia once told me that she soaks
her menorah in hot water every night
after the lighting so that the wax comes off
easy and I imagine her now
pulling her pristine menorah

from a suburban cupboard, a chicken
in the oven, the children setting the table,
how this year I will tell her about Judith,
her knife puckered against Holofernes' neck,
how I think of this as I'm chipping away

with my own.
Not a general, but nonetheless a man who believed in
the taking. When people ask me about the assault,
I say I was lucky, no bruises or marks, no tell-tale
signs visible. Only shadows and fingerprints

in my mind, does the wax become his flesh?
(it does not).

It is a miracle because of us,
our sages teach, this holiday,
our Judith saving us from those laws
of the first night. In the text it was in Latin,
the word rape a whisper tangled in the threads

of syllables, and even now, after
I've recited the blessings, I still wonder
what difference it makes in the world, a woman
lighting candles in her room alone, how safe
is she at home?

BEFORE THIS

Before this I was at my daughter's house
she has problems and sometimes
you think she is her problems
that's all she is but
I tell you she is more than her problems
and before that I was at home in my sunroom
built with money my mother left me
and before that I had a mother
who wanted me to call her
but I didn't
and before that I was in a bad marriage
as if a marriage is a country
or a neighborhood and you move
and find yourself a better one
and before that I had a slim waist
I had a filigree earbob given by a cheapskate
who told me a long story about how special it was
and before that I believed what anyone told me
and before that I splashed
in the Keya Paha River with my friends
and went home to eat doughnuts
my mother made home-made doughnuts
do you know how good that is?
and before that I was a cream puff my grandfather
stuck his finger into
on Wednesday nights when my grandmother
went into the town
and before that I was a seed, a lovely seed
like a cottonwood seed,
having my own small fluff for a parachute
floating from a great height
or maybe I was
yes I think I was an oriole's song.

Silence

Writing is hard when what you want to say makes you afraid
to remember what made you afraid, afraid of what you knew
was terrible, afraid that if you told something terrible would happen,
which was what you were told would happen when it happened,
afraid you would be punished for what happened, which certainly was your fault,
you were told, because what happened would never have happened had it not been for you,
and had never happened before. Writing is hard inside silence,
words go round and round and fall away, out of sight, out of mind,
as for years you went round and round inside silence, sentenced to this.

Writing is hard when what you want to say breaks you open
again, anger breaks open, makes you afraid, even now he's dead, that what you want to say
will break the wall between you and them, the ones you love who could not
for the life of them suspect what you know happened, would not believe
you, certainly would not believe it of him, and anyway
if it did happen, well, it was oh so long ago, why bring it up now, though a voice
you've always heard saying get away from this, take yourself away,
which you did, now warns you that frail young neighbor, who barely leaves her house,
sometimes can't think, won't hear this or that, snail in a shell, oh so brittle,
you wonder, looking at her, did it happen again, to her,
and if it did, do you need to speak, for her, death
breaking you free, if only to say something, if only you could find the words.

The Body Impolitic

Peak District, England, 1995

I set some record that year
with my rest stop requests,
marriage on life support,
the ex & I in a beat up Mini,
Sour Times on cassette EP spooling
on what was the only godsend
of that year-long trip: sound system
that cancelled conversation . . . .

       A singer crooned through
       sampled bars & beats
       End the vows no need to lie, enjoy
       Take a ride, take a shot now . . .
A long one, really, this ride or even that
we'd raise this child happily, together.

Hugging curves & hairpin turns,
we traveled on as moorland
laced with drystone walls
gave way to coal smoke & cobblestoned towns—
Ashbourne, Bakewell, Buxton, Leek,
the village markets where I bought books,
distinctive cakes or cheese (impolitic? Such appetite!).
The car would overheat, throw steam—each outing
brought some misadventure.

       Not bad, he said,
       as the souvenir rat bobbled on the rear-view
       mirror, *not bad to have puked at the plague*
       museum. I'd snapped
photos of stones drilled to hold coins
soaked in medieval disinfectant—vinegar
brining the payment for a dwindling village's
food supplies. Back on the winding road

I begged another stop. So there *in the welcoming heart*
of the nation, in some dimly remembered town,
the walls of the public loo were plastered
with porn, the peeling pages of skin mags
the anorexic bleached blondes' orange-tinted
airbrushed tan & practiced gaze
suggestive, always, of utmost *oblige*—
black markered, stained, & slashed through.

No sign of those who plied their trade or were
plied into trade, no visible trace of the hands
who slashed graffitied, bore down
an imprint of heat & hate. Thirteen
years on, my girl child's nearly a woman.
Walks further from me & into the world.

> *Eight months gone, prepared with midwife,*
> *ante-natal class, & all those Mama manuals.*
> *I was, I thought, good & ready.*

CANNIBAL WOMEN IN THE AVOCADO JUNGLE OF DEATH

They say it's the iron in the blood that resists transformation.
It is also said that no creature can learn that which his heart has no shape to hold.
When she left him alone he found women who douched,
women with eel-skin legs and simpler schedules,
women obsessed with pumice and Q-Tips.

It is said that she lay in bed three days and two nights while her body slept off
enough pills to kill a horse and he entered her regularly, and on the third day she
awoke to the sound of water breaking and left her bed to begin a new life.
The best casserole in the world has no avocado. Therefore the following is written:
>   1. Chop some leftover meat.
>   2. Cook some noodles.
>   3. Sauté some onion and green pepper.
>   4. Mix it all together with a can of Campbell's Cream of Something Soup
>   and a small amount of horseradish.
Bake at 350 degrees for one hour.
(Do not forget the horseradish or the casserole will be ordinary.)

There were nights of apple pies made with macs from upstate and enough cinnamon to make your cry. Days of attic living on Maple down the street from the folks
with the Disney characters on their front lawn and the artificial deer. Near the river
where you could see the nuclear power plant and get the willies thinking about it.
And Bear Mountain where they went on their first date and she couldn't wait to
have sex with a man who made love as if his life depended on pleasing her and it
did.

It is written that only a pig can see the wind and that wind is red.

Cannibal women in the avocado jungle of death step from behind the waterfall and
their breasts are enormous. You could hide in those breasts for days, thinking only
of guacamole. (Add chopped tomatoes, cloves of garlic crushed beneath a pestle
made of stone, juice of a lemon, and you have the kind of guacamole men die for.)

He thought: casseroles, chipped beef, shrimp if you can get it.

She thought: guacamole—and disappeared like garlic into avocado, piquant as
death, quiet as the whoosh of creation.

A Story of Stonewall

June 27, 1969, NYC

A story of Stonewall goes like this: On the night of Judy Garland's funeral I was being raped by a man I'd married at Christmas in white velvet. It was something he would never remember, the kind of incident Judy would have endured in a haze of booze, ossified from the waist down, goofy the moment before, as if the bankruptcy rumors were all true. The amazing thing was his penis—tiny and senseless, it went in and out like a needle and what was I doing this whole time? *This is the end of my dreams,* I would have thought dramatically, and it was. After the hive of gays exploded on the city and, even though Judy was laid in state, I continued straight for nineteen years. Some men think she was special, misunderstood the way they were, all that dandruff you can say about a star who dies thin and fingered as a Kleenex. To me she will always be the leader of wind and slipper, the child who scraped jelly from a jar with a dull knife, a proud moustache of milk.

BACK AND FORTH

It's his fourth sober year. I was his
good time girl: Pabst Blue Ribbon
and a baggie of Northern Lights,

the stern of his father's docked yacht,
its moon-pulled whoosh and tug,
the dark harbor lit with phosphor.

He's a boat captain now,
just married. His mother's
in remission, mine's a rummy.

As he spoke, I thought of that time
we were crawling through Miami at rush hour,
the dog that got hit then hit then hit.

I didn't know then it was a vision
of the night to come, when snuggling turned
to sex, my mute no—

he entered me, powder-soft,
pill-blind, under the black light
of his saltwater tank. I watched

the young nurse shark he caught
that summer glide back and forth,
search for an exit and snails,

her skin tough as sandpaper,
sluggish, remoraed, nocturnal,
biding her time.

Memorial Day

He left me with a hundred unpacked boxes
too heavy to lift up the rented stairs,
the baby, fussy with yeast, just beginning
to teethe, her first round of ear infections
coming on. The only calls the bill collectors',
only bills in the mail, and shiny magazines
filled with pottery I wanted but couldn't buy.
I didn't eat for two days so my dogs could.

This was after the fifth kicked garbage can,
the kitchen a mess hall of spilled beans
and coffee grounds, after the hard right
to the ear, the rug burn, the bitten fingers.
After the crushed turtle under his boot.
I wanted to go back to Mississippi many times.
I had too many dogs, cats, a newborn.
He threatened to kill who I left behind.

Tonight he'll get a hero's *hip, hip, hooray!*
down at Schooner Wharf, at the old bait
and tackle where he'll gas up his new outboard.
He'll wear a camouflage cap and his Ford
will sport ribbons and bands of honor.
A reporter from *The Citizen* interviews him
for the paper, a reward for his purple heart.

"The heart is barely recognizable"
[-autopsy report]

I told you to quit everything's a mess how many times do I have to
tell you not to buy the cheap gas this tastes like shit you treat me like
I'm five it's my kid too it's your kid what more do you want me to do
you said you would call you were supposed to call I said don't call me
on duty from base baby at home why aren't you home when did you
get home what do you have on where have you been where'd you get
that I've never seen that I saw you a donkey dick could see how you
want to be with him with her you smell like whiskey boot black sweat
you look like a harrier in that dress whore doll stop making that noise
with your mouth because you tear me up inside when you lie beside
me you look like the sky so beautiful I could job out an eye.

The Young Girl Wears Male Underwear

I saw the best minds of my generation
ridiculed on *The Lucy Show*, punished,
not for working (when did women not work?)
but for dreaming of decent jobs. Till the '60s, witches,
twitching their noses, were burned. *Samantha,*
I'm your husband. Don't be more than me.
The young girl tells me: *The rules are still theirs:*
How your body should be, how not to be aggressive.
Excuse me. Fuck that.

As a young woman, pretty, I knew their hatred,
masked as sex; was attacked and ridiculed for being smart.
I am listening, listening hard. I remember:

> *I had a neighbor, the young girls knew her*
> *she wore a red dress*
> *he hit her she spit her teeth*
> *she hid the redness*
> *beneath a sheath;*
> *for her pain*
> *there was no redress.*

The young girl tells me: *L, there was a time for*
Charlie's Angels and I Dream of Jeannie.
Not now. I can't wear high heels that will tear up my feet,
for the privilege of giving
some guy a blow job, a guy who will leave me
for someone who looks cuter in the shoes.

> I sort my wash today, wearing high heels
> and a low-cut red slung dress, frightened, and folding
> a young girl's male underwear.

CORRECTIVE RAPE (OR, I'M HERE TO HELP)

—for millicent gaika and all of our sisters

you won't know it's you in the mirror : it'll make you normal : you won't stick
out like a black eye : think of it as a kind of out-patient surgery : you'll be
more like god intended : expect to require a brief recovery period : you deserve
this : it gets rid of irregularities : you'll be right as rein(ed) : this procedure
may hurt a little : you'll feel so much better about yourself : i'll fix it so you
come correct

AT THE MUSÉE DE L'HOMME

at the *musée de*
l'homme an exhibit called *femmes du*
monde is on displayed legs shaved vulvas announce
no peace no pussy from la city of angels one imagines that beneath
their light blue chadris the women of afghanistan are also as bare as
the day they were borne bearing psychic scars after cleansing the darfurian
refugees the hutu the tutsi they cover with floral scarves wrap themselves in
fabric bearing the words *stop the violence against women* did she or the photographer
who *pays his women* the going european modeling rates choose to position this printed
protest across her derrière apropos of the brazilian cut bikinis of women in cali and sao
paulo *les femmes* as tourist attractions mutilations cut the pleasure of african women in half
but afford the men of the museum another opportunity to view the clitoris disappearing
like saartjie baartman's at long last the smile of the indigenous tahitian woman who comes
right out of a gaugin with lips and breasts plumping round and firm from her youthful body
decorated with painted designs as intricate as the hairstyles the mauritanian twins in nouak-
chott change like costumes to match their moods like the messages on the t-shirts of the all-girl
punk band in beijing screaming in english *have rock* and *deeds not words* from passion to politics
and the critique the aboriginal australian artist spits of the white man(her broker)'s greed demanding more than 50 percent of the selling price of her works because it's his market and
her/their/women's place in it is lying on a bed on a cot on a mat on the floor always hori-
zontal be they lawyers soldiers princesses prostitutes actors activists or acrobats on five
continents in dozens of countries in the world the women are lying down down for the
men the men of the many museums museums that bring them back to the drawing
board and hold them still for the camera the visitor the voyeur the man even
the woman of the north-south-east west who will leave this exhibit feeling at best equal parts desire and disgust for the sad and sexy and
vulnerable and plaintive and open and helpless and
inviting and inaccessible and yours for the
taking as book or dvd

Sonnet for My Daughter at 9

Scared of sonnets, though I never did one,
Skipped most hard parts: science, math—
So when her homework turns hard, I hum
My old song of triumph—and its aftermath—

I did not sing my childhood as a tragedy—
Had no words then, so I'd never dare
Failing. And now I face my past postfactly—
Admitting there was never anyone there.

By nine I'd been raped at least once, as I've said,
In letters that float across my brain and bounce—
Watched him on top of her as she said no in red—
I still see all of this, despite years in and out

Of therapy. See, if after this I can do a sonnet,
You can, too: Hear the silence. And then sing above it.

SPLITTING WOOD

It was the thought of his entering
their infant's room that drove her.

She remembered his face the first time
she saw him. Now, half gone from whiskey,
eyes hooded like a hawk's,
he said he'd kill the children when he woke.

The neighbors heard it,
the screams. They heard.

His workman's hand,
his gnarled hand dangled down.
The knife lay by the bed.
She slipped from the covers
while he slept, placed her feet
on the floorboards just so.

The dogs barked outside, snapdragons,
flowered tongues, and all the wired
faces of the past strung up. The ax
hung on the porch, woodpile nearby,
each log plotted, uneasily entwined.
The children's tears were rain,
tears were watering the parched hills.

The wild moon foamed at the mouth.
The wild moon crept softly at her feet.

The arms that grabbed the ax
were not her own,
that hugged it to her heart
while he slept were not hers,
the cold blade sinking in his skin.
She grew up in the country splitting wood.
She knew just how much it took
to bring a limb down.

Bat Mitzvah Lessons with the Cantor

Nothing the rabbi says is true.
A twelve-year-old girl is a half-written book.

I belong to you.
My haftora is about leprosy, dead or oozing skin,

how touch can ruin a person.
Then she must wear a bell and chant, unclean, unclean.

You choose me for my awkwardness
in my new body, choose me over the popular ones with sharp,

expensive clothes and loud laughter, choose me
for my breasts and my silence.

Mighty in black robes, you chant each line,
commanding me to copy,

broad hands on my abdomen
to guide my breath. When you lock

your office door, I shut my eyes,
pretend to be rock.

Bones jut from a lime-green dress.
Hollow-eyed, I wobble

in heels to the bimah.
The sanctuary's filled, my parents

beam from the front row. You hover
behind me as my voice shakes

and I lose my place in the prayers.
The rabbi says I'm done with childhood

now, a woman,
lovely in the eyes of God.

Nude with puzzle piece

Look for ground colors
in the corners usually
these are the corner pieces
usually the coroner will look
under her fingernails
for other pieces.

The one she is holding
is blue she was trying
to hold a straight-edged cut
of estuary.

Nude with circular saw

She wanted to circumscribe be
circumscribed it's circumstantial
that letter he left in the hole he left
in her body that said he just wanted
her to open up he wanted to open her
wanted to fill her with water the river
flooded that afternoon.

It turns out the body
is hemispherical and responds
well to division.

Port Arthur, 1939

> *The past, wrecked accordion, plays on, its one tune*
> *My song, its one breath my breath,*
> *The square root, the indivisible cipher...*
> —Charles Wright, "Sky Valley Rider"

Milly—my name, ring of sea glass, scar
crimping a wrist, O of your obituary—
oh Mother, lips purpled in death—

on the examiner's table, belly split open like a prayer book, last
gesture of your body: leaking fluids down the drainage
gutter. Pale feet, little nails.

Afternoon light lost in palm tops, wind dragging
its rusty blade back into earth. We crossed
Pier Bridge, the mainland stapled to Pleasure Island,
spit of land dredged from the sludge of the bay.
Drums of oil refineries rising like old
bones, sad tope. I held your hand, Mother—

sudden rain loping toward the future, your scarf
floating over me. The roller coaster I didn't
want to ride, its twisted vertebrae splintering the sky. You
clutched me under your arm through our slow

rise and terrifying fall, sandpipers and terns spotting
the beach like blood on an old bandage, then
night, its onslaught. You bought a ticket
to the dance hall. I waited on a bench out back,

enthralled with the blink of blue neon. When you reeled
me home—*he* was there. You slapped me, said call him *Daddy*, empty
gin bottles, the slip and smack of sweat on his face, yesterday's
ironing undone. That day fired from the dredge,
the *Mobile*, he hurled insults: me, little churl, and you, Mama, queen
of whoredom, he grabbed the iron and struck
your belly, your head. You could not call
my name with a double fractured jaw, but it goes on and on,
your voice beating out its only song.

In Mammoth September

Steps above the expressway
   she no one hires first,
they want the young student
      w/good command of basic English
to clean the loft or snip strings from jackets.
The woman on the overpass suffers changing weather,
folds unfolds her legs
on off a bus every day
   stands on hot asphalt to be or not
selected by strangers who walk up & offer
day-pay. Noon she vanishes
after swift negotiations, 20 cents below Minimum. Space
she took on the Brooklyn-Queens Expressway
is a sliver pattern
I'm living in my mind, can't get out
pattern, mothers
fight for their kids 20 cents below Minimum.
I'm here to give a poetry reading,
I told her this, woman I met
while waiting for a bus in mammoth
September's 88 degree morning.
We were trying to talk to each other,
Polish, English, reverse, start over.
One time she ended up in the wrong
building, elevator with a stuck
emergency button & a day-boss
twice her size. I asked but knew better.

ENTERING

—for Vera, in search of the sheela-nagig (ancient Irish vulva) in Rome

I feel the curvature, but barely;
entering the city on stone cold radials
                that stretch & extend themselves
          out from the cervix of the center
          among thousands of centers, I look up

high along a balustrade the ancient carved almond, *mandorla,*
the almond-slit, *vesica piscis,*
    the death-woman opens her legs & holds,

so all see while they're walking & looking up
the open muscles & lips
casting (what?)

down on smartcars, buses, bikes, carts, wheelbarrows
the swollen massive rosettes of the birther-to-all-men
lifecunt dripping onto
streetcars' silver-hot tracks—

once young women squatted over the open furrows:
                Bountiful harvest

My own yoni heart
    sheening itself with so much touching:
   moist tentacles of the vicoli I twist inside of

I nod to the old woman almond
    crumbling;
                  above, a fresh tag:
                    Stop beating women

This walk my feet were made for:
    the flight, bag, coat I dropped
                coming back to the Via Giulia

on a Monday morning in May
                moving past the excavations &
displays of the dead

INSIDE A HOUSE WITH RED DOORS

It's so easy to abuse a child.
Do you know how easy?
Pick up that wholesome avocado
from the blue porcelain bowl
by the stove and gently,
ever so gently squeeze it,
prod it with your fingers, test it
to see if it's really ripe
then set it back amid
the apples and pears, save it
for tomorrow or the next day
and forget.

Next week, when you peel away
the thick skin you will see
the fallen spots, fresh hollows
just the size of your fingertips.
Will you curse the green flesh
for the dark bruises spreading
to embrace the core of the fruit
you thought would be so delicious?

Locked tight in your own safe house,
you imitate the green grocer,
meaty hands kneading fresh fruits,
the soiled apron of your tongue, your
breeding elephant lips, your catechism
the hard crescents of your fingernails
wedged between the rug's silk tufts.

Nothing to See Here

The girl takes a bus across town
to the Pan de Vida and buys
a rosary. On the return trip
she crimps the brown beads in her palm
and pretends she is a Catholic.

She imagines herself on pilgrimage to Cologne,
peering into the hearts of 11,000 virgins.

She wants to see the tsunami
of ribs, shoulder blades, and femurs—the riot
of relics resting in the basilica. Pray
to St. Ursula's martyred handmaids:

touch the skull caps of twenty virgins
say ten Hail Marys
and you get to start over—

her body unspoiled, her body
never pressed against damp dirt
in a wide field, bluestem grass waving
a secret fortress around bare skin.

She imagines a priest feeding her apple strudel,
wrapping her in red cloth.

She ponders the logistics of beheading 11,000 girls:
How many Huns did it take? How much blood,
how long?

The Part-Time Teacher Sometime Fears for Her Students' Lives

The part-time teacher sometimes has her students read their English IA papers in front of class. She has not read them yet. She asks for volunteers.

A beautiful woman stands before the class and reads a paper in which she states that her husband beat her, and not only beat her, but hid in their house, and stalked her like prey in the jungle. The class is very silent, and she reads how she was pushed through a window, and forgave her husband in the hospital as blood streamed down her arm. She said she could not feel a thing; she had made herself a piece of wood, like Celie in *The Color Purple*, when Mr. beat her. She had made herself a piece of wood.

And she was white and middle class and had a good job, she said, and a child. And he was white and middle class and had a good job. Their friends all loved them as the perfect couple, and he stalked her at night if his socks weren't in a row in his drawer.

She saw a shrink who placed an image in her head. She was not wood; she was a pitcher of milk poring out her contents. And he asked her how long her liquid love, her rich flowing milk could pour into her man—for her lifetime (which might be short), for a year, for a month? And she poured herself out till she was dry. It took a very short time. Then she left him.

The part-time teacher knows that some women write to save their lives. The part-time teacher knows that some women speak to save their lives, and their sisters' lives.

What Do I Say to a Poet Friend
Whose Husband Has Just Died

but I know some intimate details
of their marriage—
She once told me
in a burst of confidence
after a group meditation
how her husband verbally
abused her as a young bride
and this continued for years
through three sons.
I wondered why
she did not she leave him
but then I thought again
about the three sons.

Her husband's punishment came much later
by the hand of God or fortune—
He suffered from a kind of Parkinson's
and with another stroke of luck
(for her at least)
aphasia.
He could no longer speak.
He could hear.
He could understand.
But he could not speak.

She was compassionate, even then.
But I secretly gloated—
He received his retribution
for all those years
when he called her *bitch, slut, whore*
for no good reason
other than he was an abuser
and she could not leave home,
this lovely woman,
poet, artist,
and mother of three fine sons.

I know she will probably
grieve his leaving
but I added at the end
of my sympathy note—
I wish you love
as you go through
this new transition in your life.
I wished I could have said,
Rejoice! You are free.

In Supermarkets in Italy, You Have to Put on Gloves to Touch the Bananas

I'm not there, though. I'm on the Lower East Side
in a bookstore where a little black dog in a skull & bones
sweater sleeps on a couch, snoring. A bookstore dog.
Whenever I come here I end up rereading the *Redefining Consent*
anarchofeminist zine, but never buy. It starts
with a female-identified female-bodied person
getting sexually assaulted in college, generic story,
so generic that it lacks verisimilitude, but then moves to this weird
personal-responsibility zone with 83 questions
you should ask yourself to find out if you're a rapist.
Number one: have you ever proceeded in a sexual situation
without prior verbal consent? Number two: if verbal
consent was given, did the person's body language or brief moments
of hesitation, intake of breath, quickening pulse,
communicate anything other than consent?
Number three: are you aware of your partner's possible abuse
history as a survivor of sexual assault or as a frat-boy perpetrator
pushing past limits set before punch, Keystone Ice, and close dancing?
It reminds me of the supermarkets in Italy: reaching
for the bananas, my host-sister slapped my hand away
and pointed to the gloves, miming. In my pidgin Italian,
even I understood what she said: *how could you have been so stupid?*

SEXUAL ASSAULT AWARENESS WEEK

found poem from jezebel.com

It's our job to carry an umbrella to avoid getting wet
but it's not our job to avoid nighttime, dark streets, and bars
to avoid getting raped. My mother disagrees. An act of man
versus an act of God: what difference does it make, she asks?
Carry your mace and your keys between your fingers,
pointed out like a claw. But what if all the time spent on telling us
what to do differently was spent on telling men, or everyone, not to rape?
The next time I'm told not to take my eyes off my drink
I'm going to print up cards that say, "To avoid perpetrating
sexual assault, be sure not to slip drugs into
anyone's else's drinks." And the next time I'm told that I should always
walk home with a friend, I'm going to hang a checklist that says
you should always walk home with a friend to avoid
sexually assaulting single women. Or single men. A buddy system
is important, or a whistle you can blow if you're afraid
you might rape someone. Think rape whistles blown in bars and bedrooms.
The feminist brigade would come running, and the person would say,
I'm sorry, I'm in this situation where I think I was trying to rape someone.
Thank God I had this whistle and you came.

Daughter Eraser

He sweeps her rubber ashes
into the wooden pencil box
clasps the tiny silver lock
carries her with him
wherever he goes

Sometimes to pass the time
he opens the box and runs
one finger through the soft
pink shavings, piles her
like a tiny sand mountain
blows the peak softly: landslide

He traces a happy face
into her dust, closes and shakes
the box, wonders whether
to sprinkle her somewhere

Where would she rather be, really?
He does not know:
there must be nowhere.
He never imagines

he does not know her well.
He made her.
He erased her.
What more is there to know?

Years After the Assault

I knew sex,
always in public, always
with straight girls, I knew
sex like a bastard,
it felt like nothing,
like asphalt. The objects
clearer than a stranger's
hands, or the ripping,
or my hair falling in a shape
like a musical triangle,
I remember my bus fare,
the book I'd been reading,
the lighter I'd stolen
from you, who'd left town,
the street that I called you from
(it was called Professor)
not the assault
or the seven days after
when the universe was made,
(my bed, unmade)
and you handed me my Sex Pistols
t-shirt, silently
front sewn up.

THE CIGARETTE

after a George Bellows lithograph

Now we come to the
war to end all wars.
This is the Belgian Series.
Sepia Earth, houses, Belgian
citizens. German soldiers with evil grins.

This is the cutting of a woman tied to a post, standing
for Woman, her hands tied to it,
her clothes stripped,
dirtied, pitted, slashed,
left breast slashed off.

This is the soldier slouched on her
floor, on the wall of his pleasure.
He's taking a break.
The corner of his mouth
curls toward her.

This is the title, "The Cigarette."
He holds it like an aperitif.
It lounges from two fingers
at the lower right corner
where he sits.

You can hardly see it,
the end like the pits
in her belly and face, except it's
lit. Small to be so significant
a fact of the whole composition.

The Warning

not making a sound   she watches the grindstone
wobbling   hung turning   him spitting not stopping
the blade laid on it   *scrape scrape   round   round*
round   made the yard bubble   like thousands of
his bees   his one hand turning the handle   his one
hand pressing the knife   *sharp shining*   on it

but *August!*   no sheep   no pigs   hanging
beheaded from the chestnut   but *here*   her
grandfather going   those hook-and-eye boots
always-brown clothes   that scratchy mustache
she followed   she could not *No!* and pebbles
looked up   grass stems too   whispered   *stay still*

and in the garage   no car   but hammers   saws
wrenches   awls   hanging from nails in their places
and wavy light   drew down   from dirty windows
wavy boxes of shining *oh!* *dirty there*   concrete   He
stood in it   mouth jerking machine   Spoke
Don't tell ever again Never Never Never say No

prick in her neck   made her look down at near
a girl near losing her head   But wait!
   she wasn't   she might   that arm
his hand pulling it   straight   was
   blooding   was white!   bone!   like animals
inside her   *too!*   and strings of muscle   *meat!*

the eyes saw it all   no word came out   couldn't
scream couldn't get up   head buzzed   and cold
hard cold   she felt it black   big   bigger than her
and hating!   and somewhere put it   near
the weeping blood like the statue of Jesus in church
safe in a box   (not telling)   ticking

FOR MY EX-HUSBAND

It begins slowly and small, like an incinerator's

fire, as it must, because no woman would

love what you became. After five years,

you would wake me in the night to interrogate

with candles, burning incense as a serum.

Whom had I seen, and when, did I

have lunch with any man? until, exhausted,

I began to understand why people may confess

to crimes. You and your psychologist—

Delusional, he said—you called it driven

mad with love. I left you anyway.

That night a year later, near Halloween,

you broke into my home and beat the man

asleep next to me until he had no face—

he left his cheek's pulp in his place as he ran

out, naked and faceless, and drove himself

away from both of us. You chose to rape me then,

dragged me by my ankles through blood and

shards of glass. Even today, I do not understand

how any man could do it or why you left me

alive, your own face contorted into nothing I

recognized; how, within minutes, you swept my

dignity, my god, the whole order of the world

as I knew it, away, how I remained imprisoned

in my own body as though it had stayed there

on the floor. After your incarceration, you visited

our child and wondered why I would not let you

kiss me good-bye. Because my skin would not

allow it. By day I cowered behind my own shoulders—

at night I dreamed of bullets. Finally, years after,

your mind let me go, but I did not believe it—

I stood squinting in the blue air as one among

the bony women who walked out of Dachau

wondering what I should do with the

shreds of woman left through every long

day that would follow, now that I could choose.

Spring Break

Jacksonville, Florida 1995

Three working class white girls in a blue cavalier. The wrong turn.
Trash everywhere. On the porch with 40s. We lock our doors.
This is not our neighborhood. Trash everywhere. A house on fire.
Burn baby burn. We lock our doors. A man running with a TV. Same block.
Trash everywhere. On the porch with 40s. Too thin women leaning
against a lamppost. This is not our neighborhood. We lock our doors.
On the sidewalk. A man. A black man beating a woman's face into the sidewalk.
A black woman. Blood on her face. Blood on the sidewalk. The same block.
He does not stop when he sees our car. *Burn baby burn*. We honk. She screams.
Blood. Trash. On the porch with 40s. The wrong turn. Blood on the sidewalk.
We stop our car. She screams. We scream. Three white girls. Blue cavalier. Wrong.
Doors locked. A man is running with a TV. Blood on our windows.
Missing teeth. Turn. A man is beating a woman's face into the sidewalk. She is
screaming. We are screaming. She stretches her arm towards the car. Her eyes are
white marbles. Down the street. A house on fire. She is spitting blood. We are
screaming. This is not our neighborhood. *Burn*. He does not stop when he sees
our car. Too thin women leaning against a lamppost. *Baby*. She is screaming.
Her arm stretches towards the car. We are screaming. *Burn*. Blood on the sidewalk.
Blood in her hair. Blood spitting. Screaming. We are screaming. A man.
A woman's face. The sidewalk. Beating. *Beating*. Her eyes white marbles.
Trash all around. The porch full of 40s. We drive off screaming.

SOME WOMEN, TAKE HEART

> *...I feel the*
> *rage of a soldier standing over the body of*
> *someone sent to the front lines*
> *without training*
> *or a weapon....*
> —Sharon Olds, "Indictment of Senior Officers"

Some women learn to take it with a stiff
upper lip, stitched up tight, standing up,
right on the kisser, in the teeth, jaw wired,
bruised cheek swollen on a clip under
the eye. Some women take it flat on
their backs, slapped in a cast, choked,
roped in a free-kill-zone, run down out
on the road, statistics for the *Times.*

Some women take it into the heart-
land, run with what they own, new job, new
home, new name in balled fists, chased across
state lines, life on the line—kicked down, kid-
napped, taken back. Some women breathe in
old dreams, slip under night covers, think
they stink on the sheets, knuckle under
enemy outposts in their minds.

Some women try to make it, fix it, get it
right, can't do anything right—beaten up,
beaten down, beaten to death between thin
walls, windows up. Some women start up
at the door slam, click of the briefcase clasp,
tinkle of ice in the glass, bourbon splashed
on the floor. Some women can't take any
more morning after sweet talk, panes out—
board it up, change the locks, bar the doors.

Some women—the ball busters, castrators,
man haters—stick out their tongues on a dare,
tear in the skin *(this is a pore war)*, go for
the muscle and scream: *no more*, bloody
spit ribboning lips, mouthy at the firing line
like they mean it. Some women take
a match to the gas, burn the bed, end up
rattling chains behind bars. Some women
want a revolution like a lover
and a full metal jacket for a heart.

THIS: A TRIPTYCH FOR THE DISAPPEARED

> *Her face has disappeared. This happens*
> *more often than you think.*
> —Andrea Hollander Budy

1.

She is six.

She is a kid

in a cowgirl suit,

strapping on a holster

at her cherry three-wheeler,

the city steed, clumps of mud

in the ring of its chain.

But it has come to this:

Twenty years later

she is on her back,

a woman dressed up

as someone's bed,

blood on the sheets.

She is the bed.

She is the ceiling.

She is the wall.

She is the room.

This has happened:

Her face disappeared

beneath the scarlet

throb of a bruise.

2.
This is the country where
nothing sells for more
than its whores, rest
and recreation for a global
economy, pedophiles reclined
behind a camouflage of pc screens,
eagerly scanning rental lists
by the hour, by the day,
by the month, for a lifetime,

the sexual slavery pimp's finger
on the trigger of the cocked
crack gun, lolitot posed
like a CK ad in a flickering
light bulb dark, catalogued
child-bride, ready-made to order,
but she is not this body. *This*
is not a good job for a poor girl.

3.
Across the sprawling green of lawn
at another dias de los muertos,
pink crosses stagger the walk
for the murdered women of Juarez,
hundreds disappeared over a decade.

A procession of candles sputter
and spark for a school house splattered
in blood, its Amish girls gunned down
by a milk truck driver with three guns
and a grudge in West Nickel Mines, PA.

Muffled prayers petition the October air
for women packed tight in shipping containers
across the Pacific Northwest, later to appear
on packing lists masked as menus, their bodies
indexed as lo mein, satay, kimchi, or pho.

Frankincense smolders for those who
vanish, shadows in the streets, whole bodies
disappearing under the weight of burqas.
It burns for all of those who are not,
for all of those who never will be.

Notes to the Poems

Christina Lovin: "Panes" March 27, 1964—Catherine Genovese, was stabbed to death near her home in New York City today while her neighbors watched. According to a *New York Times* report, the killer made three attacks spread out over more than 30 minutes, during which 38 people watched. Not one of the bystanders helped the young woman or called for help, either saying they "didn't want to get involved" or they had been too afraid to call the police.

Evie Shockley: "corrective rape (or, i'm here to help)" "According to a report by international group ActionAid, 10 new cases of lesbians being raped are reported every week in Cape Town alone…"—Paula Brooks, for LezGetReal, 4/4/10.

Judith Vollmer: "In Mammoth September" *for my Rzeszow cousins*, and with gratitude for Nina Bernstein's story, "Hungry for Work, Immigrant Women Gather on Corners and Hope for the Best," *New York Times*, 8/15/2005.

Acknowledgements

I would also like to thank Adam Wagler, Rachel Brown Abraham, Lisa Wagler, and Sally Brown Deskins. I would also like to thank my students, teachers, and colleagues at the University of Nebraska-Lincoln. I want to thank the Jacht Club Lab, especially Amy Struthers. I want to thank those involved with Women's Week, No Limits, Tuesday with Writers, One Billion Rising, 100 Thousand Poets for Change, and Poetry at the Moon. I want to thank all the women who were my poetry students in the poetry workshops at a local crisis center.

My gratitude to everyone at Hyacinth Girl Press, especially Margaret Bashaar.

The first draft of the critical introduction was written as the term project for a class in American poetry taught by Dr. Kenneth Price at the University of Nebraska-Lincoln in 2008. It draws from other critical essays, specifically essays I wrote during my M.A. and Ph.D. studies at the University of Arizona and at UNL, and an essay written by Dr. Christine Stewart-Nunez during her Ph.D. studies at UNL. Dr. Stewart-Nunez delivered an excerpt from this introduction in a panel I chaired and at which I presented: "Listening for Silences: Resisting Hegemonic Narratives of Violence," National Women's Studies Association conference, Cincinnati, Ohio, June 2008. I am indebted to Dr. Sara Spurgeon for her assistance in my thinking through ideas of victims, survivors, and fighters, to Dr. Stewart-Nunez for her mentoring while we were both graduate students at UNL and her early guidance in this project, for Dr. Amelia Montes for her assistance in my thinking through ideas of resistance, and my other teachers, mentors, and friends who offered support, guidance, and feedback Hilda Raz, Ken Price, Joy Castro, Barbara DiBernard, Helen Moore, Amy Goodburn, Kwame Dawes, and Grace Bauer.

Finally, grateful acknowledgement is made to the generous poets and publishers who granted permission to print and/or reprint the poems in this anthology. Unless specifically noted otherwise, copyright of the poem is held by the individual poets.

Lucy Adkins: "Grandmother Ellen Tells it Like it Was" first appeared in *Plainsongs*, 2001. It also appeared in the anthology *Times of Sorrow/Times of Grace* (The Backwaters Press, 2002) and *Pudding Magazine: The International Journal of Applied Poetry*, No. 49, 2002. "Rat" first appeared in *South Dakota Review*, Vol. 41, 2003 and from *One Life Shining, Addie Finch Farmwife*, by Lucy Adkins and published by Pudding House Publications, © 2007 by Lucy Adkins. Printed with permission of the author.

Kathleen Aguero: "Medusa" from *Daughter Of* by Kathleen Aguero and published by Cedar Hill Books, © 2005 Kathleen Aguero. Reprinted by permission of the author.

Amanda Auchter: "Creole Tomatoes," copyright © 2012 by Amanda Auchter is reprinted from *The Wishing Tomb*, with the permission of Perugia Press, Florence, MA (www.perugiapress.com).

Lana Hechtman Ayers: "Traife" from *Dance From Inside My Bones* by Lana Hechtman Ayers and published by Snake Nation Press, © 2007 by Lana Hechtman Ayers. Reprinted with permission of the author.

Wendy Barker: "Why I Dread Teaching *The Sun Also Rises*" first appeared in *Mid-American Review*, 28, No. 2, 2007.

Hadara Bar-Nadav: "My Wife in All Things" first appeared in *The American Poetry Review* 40.6 (2011) and "Lust and Smoke" first appeared in *Beloit Poetry Journal* 57.4 (2007). Both poems from *The Frame Called Ruin* by Hadara Bar-Nadav and published by New Issues Poetry & Prose, © 2012 by Hadara Bar-Nadav. Reprinted with permission of the author.

Ellen Bass: "Bearing Witness" from *Mules of Love*. Copyright © 2002 by Ellen Bass. Reprinted with the permission of The Permissions Company, Inc. on behalf of BOA Editions, Ltd., www.boaeditions.org.

Elliott batTzedek: "Wanting A Gun" first appeared in *Trivia: Voices of Feminism*, Issue 6, September 2007.

Lois Marie Harrod: "Off" first appeared in *Iris: A Journal about Women*, 39, Fall 1999.

Allison Hedge Coke: "No, I am not a Vet: *Quincentennial Poem*, 7-7-92" first appeared in *Skin Deep: Women Writing on Color, Culture and Identity*, edited by Elena Featherstone The Crossing Press, 1994. "shapings" first appeared in *Poets Against the War*, edited by Sam Hamill, 2003.

Janis Butler Holm: "Pulp Nonfiction" first appeared in *Tessera*, Vol. 37-38 (Fall 2005).

Julie Kane: "Mockingbird" from *Jazz Funeral* by Julie Kane and published by Story Line Press, © 2009 by Julie Kane. Reprinted with permissions of the author and Story Line Press.

Susan Kelly-DeWitt: "Pomegranates" first appeared in *Hawaii Review*, Fall 1994, Issue 42, Vol. 18, No. 3. "Whisky Nights" first appeared in *Prairie Schooner*, Winter 2006. Bot from *The Fortunate Islands* by Susan Kelly-DeWitt and published by Marick Press, © 2008 by Susan Kelly-DeWitt. Reprinted with permission of the author.

Alexis Krasilovsky: "Inanna in Iraq" originally appeared in the DVD, *Some Women Writers Kill Themselves: Selected Videopoems and Poetry of Alexis Krasilovsky* (Rafael Film: Los Angeles, 2007).

Wendi Lee: "Portraits of Marriage" first appeared in *Plainsongs*, Vol. XXVIII, No. 1 and from *Knotted Ends* by Wendi Lee, © 2012 by Wendi Lee and published by Finishing Line Press. Reprinted with permission of the author and Finishing Line Press.

Lisa Lewis: "The Accident" from *The Unbeliever* by Lisa Lewis and published by University of Wisconsin Press, © 1994 by Lisa Lewis. Reprinted with permission of the author and University of Wisconsin Press. "Tracy and Joe," first appeared in Stand Up Poetry, 2002, and from *Vivisect* by Lisa Lewis and published by New Issues Press, © 2010 by Lisa Lewis. Reprinted with permission of the author and New Issues Press.

Ellaraine Lockie: "Ode to an Ex" first appeared in *The New Orphic Review*, 2003.

Christina Lovin: "Panes" first appeared in *Poetry Quarterly* (2010).

Alison Luterman: "Another Vigil at San Quentin" first appeared in *The Sun* and from *See How We Almost Fly* by Alison Luterman and published by Pearl Editions, © 2010 by Alison Luterman. Reprinted with permission of the author.

Marie-Elizabeth Mali: "Anglerfish" first appeared in *The New Verse News*, May 2011, and "A Grapple of Sparrows" first appeared in *Connotation Press: An Online Artifact*, April 2012.

Linda McCarriston: "Grateful" first published in *The Seneca Review*, XXI, #1, 1991 and "To Judge Faolain, Dead Long Enough: A Summons" first published in *The Boston Review*, June, 1987. Both poems from *Eva-Mary* by Linda McCarriston, © 1991 by Linda McCarriston and published by Northwestern University Press. Reprinted with permission of the author and Northwestern University Press.

Dawn McGuire: "A Grecian Ode" first appeared in *The Aphasia Café* by Dawn McGuire and published by IFSF Publishing, © 2012. Reprinted with permission of the publisher.

Leslie Adrienne Miller: "Gautier D'Agoty's Écorchés" first appeared in *Prairie Schooner*, 79:2, Summer 2005 and from *The Resurrection Trade* by Leslie Adrienne Miller and published by Graywolf Press, © 2007 Leslie Adrienne Miller. "Rough Music, Edinburgh 1829" from *The Resurrection Trade* by Leslie Adrienne Miller and published by Graywolf Press, © 2007 Leslie Adrienne Miller. Reprinted with permission of the author.

Contributors' Biographies

Kristin Abraham is the author of two poetry chapbooks: *Little Red Riding Hood Missed the Bus* (Subito Press, 2008), and *Orange Reminds You of Listening* (Elixir Press, 2006); her poetry, lyric essays, and critical writing have appeared in numerous journals and literary magazines, including *Best New Poets 2005, Court Green, Columbia Poetry Review, The Journal, LIT,* and *American Letters & Commentary*. She teaches at Laramie County Community College in Wyoming and serves as co-founder, managing editor and poetry editor of the literary magazine *Spittoon*.

Lucy Adkins grew up in rural Nebraska, attended country schools, and received her degree from Auburn University in Alabama. Her poetry has been published in journals which include the *Owen Wister Review, Nebraska Territory, Northeast, South Dakota Review, Concho River Review,* and the anthologies *Woven on the Wind, Times of Sorrow/Times of Grace, Crazy Woman Creek,* and the *Poets Against the War* anthology. Her chapbook, *One Life Shining: Addie Finch, Farmwife* was published in 2007 by Pudding House Press.

Kathleen Aguero's poetry collections include *Investigations: The Mystery of the Girl Sleuth, Daughter Of, The Real Weather* and *Thirsty Day*. She has also co-edited three volumes of multi-cultural literature for the University of Georgia Press and is poetry editor of *Solstice Literary Magazine*. She teaches at Pine Manor College in both the undergraduate and low-residency M.F.A. programs and in Changing Lives through Literature, an alternative sentencing program.

Carol Alena Aronoff, Ph.D.: psychologist, teacher, writer. Her poetry appears in *Comstock Review, Potpourri, Poetic Realm, Poetica, Mindprints, In Our Own Words, HeartLodge, Out of Line, Sendero, Buckle&, Iodine, Asphodel, Nomad's Choir, New Verse News, Avocet, Tiger's Eye,* several anthologies, etc. She received a prize in the *Common Ground* poetry contest, was a Pushcart Prize nominee, participated four times in Braided Lives, collaboration of artists/poets. *The Nature of Music,* was published in 2005, *Cornsilk,* in 2006, *Her Soup Made the Moon Weep,* in 2007. *Blessings From an Unseen World* will be published soon. Dr. Aronoff resides in rural Hawaii.

María Luisa Arroyo has published poems in journals, including *Calyx* and *Palabra*. Her first collection of poems, *Gathering Words: Recogiendo Palabras* (The Bilingual Review, ASU: 2008) "… speaks from battered women's shelters and from inside homes that hide domestic violence and child abuse." María Luisa's poetry workshops include "The Power of Code-Switching: Poems Don't Have to Be 'English Only'" at the 2012 Split This Rock Poetry Festival. With acclaimed playwright, Magdalena Gómez, María Luisa co-edited the anthology, *Bullying: Replies, Rebuttals, Confessions, Catharsis*.

Amanda Auchter is the editor of Pebble Lake Review and the author of two books of poetry: *The Wishing Tomb,* winner of the 2012 Perugia Press Award, and *The Glass Crib,* winner of the 2010 Zone 3 Press First Book Award. She lives in Houston, Texas and teaches Creative Writing and Composition at Lone Star College.

Lana Hechtman Ayers, originally from New York, made her way to the Pacific Northwest via New Hampshire where she obtained an MFA in Poetry from New England College and a Masters in Counseling from Antioch. Lana works as a poetry manuscript consultant and writing workshop facilitator. She runs two chapbook presses, *Concrete Wolf* and *MoonPath Press*. Lana is author of two chapbooks and three full-length poetry collections. Her most recent collection, *A New Red* (Pecan Grove Press, 2010), is a contemporary feminist re-imagining of the Red Riding Hood fairy tale.

Wendy Barker has published five collections of poetry and three chapbooks, most recently, *Nothing Between Us* (Del Sol Press, 2009) and *Things of the Weather* (Pudding House, 2009). Other books include a selection of poems with accompanying essays, *Poems' Progress* (Absey & Co., 2002), and a collection translated in collaboration with Saranindranath Tagore, *Rabindranath Tagore: Final Poems* (Braziller, 2001). Her poems have appeared in *Poetry, Georgia Review, Southern Review,* and

Gettysburg Review. Recipient of NEA and Rockefeller fellowships, she is Poet-in-Residence and the Pearl LeWinn Endowed Professor of Creative Writing at the University of Texas at San Antonio.

Hadara Bar-Nadav is the author of *A Glass of Milk to Kiss Goodnight* (Margie/Intuit House, 2007), awarded the Margie Book Prize, and *The Frame Called Ruin* (New Issues, 2012), Runner Up/Editor's Selection for the Green Rose Prize. Her chapbook, *Show Me Yours* (Laurel Review/GreenTower Press, 2010), was awarded the 2009 Midwest Poets Series Award. Bar-Nadav is currently Assistant Professor of English and Director of Creative Writing at the University of Missouri-Kansas City.

Ellen Bass's poetry books include *The Human Line* (Copper Canyon, 2007) and *Mules of Love* (BOA, 2002). Among her awards are a Pushcart Prize, the Lambda Literary Award, The Pablo Neruda Prize, *New Letters* Prize, and Larry Levis Award from *Missouri Review*. Her poems have been published in *The Atlantic, The Kenyon Review, American Poetry Review, The New Republic* and many other journals. She co-edited the first major anthology of women's poetry *No More Masks!* with Florence Howe (Doubleday, 1973) and co-authored *The Courage to Heal* with Laura Davis. She teaches in the MFA program at Pacific University. www.ellenbass.com

Elliott batTzedek holds an MFA in Poetry and Poetry in Translation from Drew University, for which she translated *Dance of the Lunatic* by the Israeli Jewish lesbian writer Shez; this manuscript won the 2012 Robert Bly Translation prize, judged by Martha Collins. Her work appears or is forthcoming in the journals *Armchair/Shotgun, Massachusetts Review, Adanna Literary Journal, Poemeleon, Trivia, Naugatuck River Review, Lambda Literary Online,* and *Sinister Wisdom,* and in the anthologies *Two Lines Translation Anthology* and *Overplay/Underdone,* and as a "Split This Rock" poem of the week.

Grace Bauer's books include *Retreats & Recognitions, Beholding Eye,* and *The Women at the Well,* as well as several chapbooks of poems. She is also co-editor of the anthology *Umpteen Ways of Looking at a Possum: Critical & Creative Responses to Everette Maddox.* Her poems, stories and essays have appeared in numerous anthologies and journals. She teaches in the Creative Writing and Women's Studies Programs at the University of Nebraska-Lincoln.

Kimberly L. Becker is a member of Wordcraft Circle of Native Writers and Storytellers and is of Cherokee/Celtic/Teutonic descent. *Words Facing East* (WordTech Editions, 2011) is her first book of poetry. Kimberly was the recipient of a 2011 Individual Artist Award in Poetry from the Maryland State Arts Council. A grant from the Arts and Humanities Council of Montgomery County (MD) funded her study of Cherokee language, history, and culture in Cherokee, NC. She has also been awarded residencies at Hambidge and Weymouth. www.kimberlylbecker.com

Laure-Anne Bosselaar is the author of *The Hour Between Dog and Wolf, Small Gods of Grief,* which won the Isabella Gardner Prize for Poetry in 2001, and *A New Hunger,* an ALA Notable Book for 2008. She edited four poetry anthologies, and translated a book of Dutch poetry: *The Plural of Happiness,* poems by Herman de Coninck. The recipient of a Pushcart Prize, she taught at Sarah Lawrence College and is on the faculty of the Low Residency MFA in Creative Writing Program of Pine Manor College. She lives in California.

Kristy Bowen runs dancing girl press & studio, an indie press and design studio based in Chicago. She is the author of several limited edition chapbook projects and three full-length books, *the fever almanac* (Ghost Road, 2006), *in the bird museum* (Dusie Press, 2008) and *girl show* (Black Lawrence Press, forthcoming 2013).

Ann Bracken is a writer, poet, educator, and expressive arts consultant whose poetry, essays, and interviews have appeared in the *Little Patuxent Review, Life in Me Like Grass on Fire: Love Poems, Praxilla, The Museletter,* and *The Gunpowder Review,* and *Reckless Writing Anthology: Emerging Poets of the 21st Century.* Her company, The Possibility Project, offers expressive arts programs for women of all ages. Ann is a lecturer in the Professional Writing Program at the University of Maryland.

Shevaun Brannigan is an MFA candidate at Bennington College. She has been previously published in such journals as *Calyx, Lumina, So to Speak, Swivel: the Nexus of Women and Wit,* and *Rattle,* which nominated her for a Pushcart Prize at age 22. She thanks her parents for their encouragement of her writing.

Susana H. Case, professor at the New York Institute of Technology, has recent work in many journals, including *Hawai'i Pacific Review, Portland Review, Potomac Review* and *Saranac Review.* She is the author of the book *Salem In Séance* (WordTech Editions, 2013) and the chapbooks *The Scottish Café* (Slapering Hol Press), *Anthropologist In Ohio* (Main Street Rag Publishing Company), *The Cost Of Heat* (Pecan Grove Press), and *Manual of Practical Sexual Advice* (Kattywompus Press). An English-Polish reprint of *The Scottish Café, Kawiarnia Szkocka,* was published by Opole University Press in Poland. http://iris.nyit.edu/~shcase/.

Joy Castro is the author of the memoir *The Truth Book,* the literary thriller *Hell or High Water,* and the essay collection *Island of Bones.* She teaches at the University of Nebraska-Lincoln.

Sarah A. Chavez is a mestiza born and raised in the California Central Valley currently making her way through academics in the Midwest. She is a fourth year PhD student in Creative Writing with a focus in poetry and Ethnic American Literature at the University of Nebraska-Lincoln. Her work can be found or is forthcoming in *Women Arts Quarterly, The Acentos Review,* and *Caylx* among others.

Meg Day is a three-time Pushcart-nominated poet, nationally awarded spoken word artist, & veteran arts educator who is currently a PhD fellow in Poetry & Disability Poetics at the University of Utah. A 2010 Lambda Fellow, 2011 Hedgebrook Fellow, & 2012 Squaw Valley Fellow, Meg completed her MFA at Mills College & publishes the femme ally zine, *ON OUR KNEES.* A 2012 AWP Intro Award Winner & nominee for the Best New Poets of 2012, Meg's work can be found in *Drunken Boat & Artful Dodge & This Assignment is So Gay: Poems from LGBTQ Teachers.* www.megday.com

Sandi Day is currently enrolled in the MFA Program at the University of Idaho in Moscow, Idaho - although as a native Californian she struggles mightily with the Idaho winters, which she says seem to last until summer. As an undergrad, Sandi studied French feminist Helene Cixous, and has since been interested in the Cixous' theory of *ecriture feminine,* or feminine writing. She is interested in reading and writing poems that express and deal with the idea of Woman and what it means to be a woman in the world.

Marylisa DeDomenicis was the 2010 recipient of the Toni Brown Memorial Scholarship. Her chapbook, *Almost All Red,* won the Still Waters Press Poetry Chapbook Competition and was nominated for a Pushcart prize. In addition, she's read for Stockton College's Visiting Writer's Series, her poems have been performed on stage (sponsored by NJSCA), published in books, a calendar, a broadside, and in various print and online publications. She is realizing her girlhood dream of living in a cottage near the ocean while writing. www.notherpoet.com/Bio.html

Mary Stone Dockery's first poetry collection, *Mythology of Touch,* was released in 2012 by Woodley Press. She is the author of *Aching Buttons* and *Blink Finch,* two forthcoming chapbooks, and her collaborative chapbook written with Katie Longofono, titled *Honey and Bandages,* will be released in 2013. She currently lives and writes in St. Joseph, MO.

Jehanne Dubrow is the author of four poetry collections, including most recently *Red Army Red* and *Stateside* (Northwestern UP, 2012 and 2010). Her work has appeared in *Southern Review, Crazyhorse, Prairie Schooner,* and *Ploughshares.* She is the Director of the Rose O'Neill Literary House and an assistant professor in creative writing at Washington College, on the Eastern Shore of Maryland.

Angele Ellis is the author of *Spared* (Main Street Rag, 2011), an Editors' Choice Chapbook Selection, and *Arab on Radar* (Six Gallery Press, 2007). A 2008 recipient of a poetry fellowship from the Pennsylvania Council on the Arts, she won Pittsburgh Filmmakers' 2009 G-20 Haiku Contest, and received third prize in the 2007 RAWI Competition for Creative Prose and honorable mention in the 2011 Shine Journal Poetry Contest.

Gail Rudd Entrekin is editor of the online environmental literary journal *Canary* and Poetry Editor of Hip Pocket Press. She has taught English Literature and Creative Writing in California colleges for over 25 years. She has published four books of poetry, the most recent being *Rearrangement of the Invisible* (Poetic Matrix Press, 2012). Her poems have been widely published in anthologies and journals, including *Cimarron Review, Nimrod, The Ohio Journal*, and *Southern Poetry Review,* and were finalists for the Pablo Neruda Prize from Nimrod in 2011.

Becky Faber has been writing since the 20th Century. Her poems have appeared in *Small Brushes, So to Speak, The Blue Collar Review, The Midwest Quarterly, The Plains Songs Review, Plainsongs,* the *Nebraska English Counselor,* and the anthologies *Nebraska Voices* and *Lyrical Iowa*. She is a career counselor at the University of Nebraska-Lincoln where she earned a PhD in English.

Rebecca Foust's fourth book, *All That Gorgeous Pitiless Song,* won the Many Mountains Moving Book Prize and was a finalist for the 2012 Poet's and Paterson Prizes. God, Seed won the 2011 Foreword Book of the Year Award, and her new manuscript was shortlisted for the 2012 Kathryn A. Morton Prize. Her recent poems are in *Hudson Review, JAMA, Notre Dame Review, Sewanee Review, Woman's Review of Books* and elsewhere, and her essays and book reviews are in current issues of *American Book Review, Calyx, Chautauqua* and *Prairie Schooner*.

Rebecca Morgan Frank is the author of the poetry collection *Little Murders Everywhere* (Salmon Poetry, 2012). Her poems have appeared in such places as *Ploughshares, The Georgia Review, Guernica, Post Road, Poetry Daily, Crazyhorse, Hawai'i Pacific Review,* and *Best New Poets 2008*. She has been awarded the Poetry Society of America's 2010 Alice Fay di Castagnola Award, an AWP Intro Journal Award, and fellowships from the Virginia Center for Creative Arts, the Writers' Room of Boston, and the Sewanee Writers' Conference. She is an assistant professor at the University of Southern Mississippi's Center for Writers.

Kerri French's poetry has been featured in Sirius Satellite Radio and has appeared in *Barrow Street, Mid-American Review, DIAGRAM, Sou'wester, Waccamaw, Barrelhouse, Lumina, Best New Poets 2008,* and *The Southern Poetry Anthology,* among others. A recipient of the Larry Franklin and Mei Kwong Fellowship from the Writers' Room of Boston, she holds degrees from Boston University, UNC-Chapel Hill, and UNC-Greensboro. A North Carolina native, she lives in Cambridge, England.

Alice Friman was named Georgia Author of the Year for Poetry, 2012. Her new collection is *Vinculum,* LSU. Her last two books are *The Book of the Rotten Daughter,* BkMk, and *Zoo,* Arkansas. New work appears in *The Georgia Review, The Gettysburg Review, Boulevard, New Letters* and the 2012 Pushcart Prize Anthology. She is Poet-in-Residence at Georgia College in Milledgeville.

Janice Moore Fuller has published three poetry collections, including *Séance* from Iris Press, winner of the 2008 Oscar Arnold Young Award (North Carolina poetry book of the year). Her poems have appeared in numerous national and international magazines, including *Magma* (London) and *New Welsh Review*. Her plays and libretti have been produced at Catawba's Hedrick Theatre, BareBones Theater's New Play Festival, the Minneapolis Fringe Festival, Estonia's Polli Talu Centre, and France's Rendez-Vous Musique Nouvelle. She has been a Fellow at artist colonies in Ireland, Scotland, Spain, and Portugal.

Megan Gannon's poems have appeared in *Ploughshares, Pleiades, Notre Dame Review, Best American Poetry 2006*, and on *Verse Daily* and *Poetry Daily*. Her chapbook, *The Witch's Index*, was published in 2012 by Sweet Publications, and her first novel, *Cumberland*, is under representation with Writer's House LLC. She lives in Omaha, Nebraska.

Gaynell Gavin is the author of *Attorney-at-Large* (Main Street Rag Publishing). MSR also published her poetry chapbook, *Intersections*. She was a finalist in the AWP Award Series for Creative Nonfiction, the 2011 Zone 3 Press Nonfiction Book Award, and the 2012 *Solstice* Prize in Nonfiction. Her fiction, creative nonfiction, and poetry appear or are forthcoming in many journals and anthologies, including *The Bellevue Literary Review, Prairie Schooner, Quercus Review, Best New Poets 2006* (Samovar Press), and *The Untidy Season* (Backwaters Press).

Gail Ghai is a poet, English/ESL teacher and workshop leader. Her poems have appeared in *Descant, JAMA, Kaliope, Poet Works, Shenandoah,* and *Yearbook of American Poetry*. Awards include a Pushcart Prize nomination and a Henry C. Frick scholarship for creative teaching. She is the author of three chapbooks of poetry.

Rain C. Goméz, (Sutton Doctoral Fellow, English University of Oklahoma) won the First Book Award in poetry for *Smoked Mullet Cornbread Memory* (under contract Mongrel Empire Press), from Native Writers' Circle of the Americas. Creative and Academic work has appeared in or is forthcoming in various journals including *Tidal Basin Review, Natural Bridge, SING: Indigenous Poetry of the Americas, Yellow Medicine Review, American Indian Culture and Research Journal,* and *Louisiana Folklife*. Her academic and poetic work is located at the intersections of Louisiana Indian (Choctaw, Houma, Tunica-Biloxi, Caddo) and Louisiana Creole (Mestiz@) textual survivance narratives within Southern Literary Studies.

Judy Grahn is widely known as a poet and cultural theorist. Her poetry fueled second wave feminist and lesbian activism, and continues to impact people world-wide. She has published five collections, eight chapbooks, and two book-length poems, much of which has been dramatized and put to music. Every year she reads parts of "women are tired of the ways men bleed" for "Guardianas de la Vida," in the Mission District of SF. She teaches and co-directs the MA in Women's Spirituality at the Institute of Transpersonal Psychology, and has an online journal: www.metaformia.org.

Therese Halscheid happened to lead a group of American women writers to South Africa to meet with African writers. There, they met an African woman, Tabs Nachinga, who was documenting women's stories, their tribal ways. Tabs shared that long ago, in old rural villages, when a man was abusive to his wife, the women would gather to create a song about his abuse and sing it openly to shame him. These songs held power and became known as "women's play things." This poem has been used to help women of abuse through the Camden County Cultural & Heritage Commission. Counselors use the poem as a stepping off point, in assisting clients.

Twyla Hansen's newest book, *Dirt Songs: A Plains Duet* (with Linda Hasselstrom), won a 2012 Nebraska Book Award and was finalist for the 2012 Willa Literary Award and the High Plains Book Award. She has five previous poetry books, including *Potato Soup*, a 2004 Nebraska Book Award winner. Her writing has appeared widely in publications such as *Prairie Schooner, Midwest Quarterly, South Dakota Review, Prairie Fire newspaper, Organization & Environment, Encyclopedia of the Great Plains, Crazy Woman Creek: Women Rewrite the American West,* and *A Contemporary Reader for Creative Writing*. Her B.S. and M.Ag. are from the University of Nebraska-Lincoln.

Lois Marie Harrod's twelfth collection *The Only Is* won the 2012 Tennessee Chapbook Contest (*Poems & Plays*), her eleventh *Brief Term*, a collection of poems about teachers and teaching was published by Black Buzzard Press, 2011, and her *Cosmongony* won the 2010 Hazel Lipa Chapbook (Iowa State). She teaches Creative Writing at The College of New Jersey. www.loismarieharrod.com

Allison Adelle Hedge Coke authored books include: (American Book Award) *Dog Road Woman* and *Off-Season City Pipe*, poetry; *Rock Ghost, Willow, Deer*, a memoir; and *Blood Run*, a verse-play that served to lobby for legislation and protection of the Indigenous site. Hedge Coke has edited eight additional collections, including *Sing: Poetry from the Indigenous Americas, Effigies, & Effigies II*. She came of age cropping tobacco and working fields, waters, and working in factories.

Sara Henning's poetry, fiction, interviews and book reviews have appeared in such journals as *Verse, So To Speak, Weave,* and *The Sow's Ear Poetry Review*. Her chapbook, *To Speak of Dahlias*, is forthcoming from Finishing Line Press. Currently a doctoral student in English and Creative Writing at the University of South Dakota, she serves as Circulations Manager for *The South Dakota Review*.

Janis Butler Holm lives in Athens, Ohio, where she has served as Associate Editor for *Wide Angle*, the film journal. Her prose, poems, and performance pieces have appeared in small-press, national, and international magazines. Her plays have been produced in the U.S., Canada, and England.

Nicole Hospital-Medina, a Florida native and second year M.F.A. poet at the University of Miami, teaches creative writing. She earned her Bachelor's in English with a minor in education at the University of North Florida where her devotion to the ocean grew. She surfed her way through college. Nicole has worked as a Track and Field coach and a sailing instructor in Biscayne Bay. She recently won the 2011 Miami Herald Haiku Challenge and has been regarded as an activist. Nicole, an explorer of the Earth and its inhabitants, finds inspiration from her experiences.

Judy Juanita's first novel will be published by Viking Press in 2013. Her poetry has appeared in *13th Moon, Painted Bride Quarterly, Lips, Rooms, Crab Orchard Review, Croton Review, Good News, Drum Revue 2000 and Obsidian II*, online in Asili the journal, Poetrymagazine.com, and *Glint*. Her plays have been produced in Oakland, San Francisco, Los Angeles, NYC's Lower East Side; at the Bay Area Playwrights Festival, SF's Off-Market Theater, and the SF Mime Troupe. Woman's Will 24-hour Playfest at the Julia Morgan Theater for the Performing Arts in Berkeley produced five of her plays from 2005-2009.

Julie Kane's most recent poetry collections are *Rhythm & Booze* (2003), Maxine Kumin's pick for the National Poetry Series and a Poets' Prize finalist, and *Jazz Funeral* (2009), the winner of the Donald Justice Poetry Prize, judged by David Mason. Currently serving a two-year term as Louisiana Poet Laureate, she teaches at Northwestern State University in Natchitoches, Louisiana.

Susan Kelly-DeWitt is the author of *The Fortunate Islands* (Marick Press, 2008), eight small press collections, and the electronic chapbook *The Limbo Suite* (Mudlark No. 38). Her work appears in many journals and anthologies, most recently *The Autumn House Anthology of Contemporary American Poetry*. She's currently a contributing editor for *Poetry Flash* and a featured blogger for *Coal Hill Review*.

Jill Khoury earned her Masters of Fine Arts from The Ohio State University. Her poems have appeared or are forthcoming in numerous journals, including *Sentence, MiPOesias, Wordgathering,* and *RHINO*. She has been nominated for the Pushcart Prize twice by *Breath and Shadow: A Journal of Disability Culture and Literature*, and has a chapbook, *Borrowed Bodies* from Pudding House Press. She blogs about poetry, disability, and art at quixotic-a.blogspot.com.

Paula Kolek is a teacher, visual artist, poet, and intertextual/multi-media fanatic. Her literary work has been published in *New Letters, Reconstruction, Collective Brightness Anthology, Ditch, Fickle Muses* among other literary journals. Her text & images, "Domino," "this is a pHOTo opportunity," and "PowerGirl," from the series *A Form of Tenderness*, were exhibited at Add Juncture, July 2011, and her intertextual book and installation exhibited at Humorarium, October 2011. Kolek currently teaches writing and literature at Miami Dade College and Barry University.

Alexis Krasilovsky's DVD *Some Women Writers Kill Themselves: Selected Videopoems and Poems* won the "Best of the Fest" Literary Award at the 2008 Austin Woman's Film, Music and Literary Festival. Her poetry has appeared in *Poetica, Southern Exposure, San Francisco Bay Guardian* and the Museum of Modern Art. She is also a contributor to the anthology *Women on Poetry*. Krasilovsky is a professor of screenwriting at California State University, Northridge and the writer/director of *Women Behind the Camera* (www.womenbehindthecamera.com) and other films.

Marianne Kunkel is the managing editor of *Prairie Schooner* and a Ph.D. student in poetry at the University of Nebraska-Lincoln, with a specialization in women's and gender studies. Her poems have appeared in *Columbia Poetry Review, Hayden's Ferry Review, Poet Lore, Rattle, River Styx,* and elsewhere, and her chapbook, *The Laughing Game,* is from Finishing Line Press.

Wendi Lee was born and raised in Honolulu, and has since lived in Kentucky, New York City, and Pittsburgh. She received her MFA from Sarah Lawrence College, and her chapbook, *Knotted Ends,* was recently published by Finishing Line Press.

Lisa Lewis' books are *The Unbeliever, Silent Treatment, Vivisect,* and *Burned House with Swimming Pool,* as well as a chapbook titled *Story Box.* She was the 2011 recipient of a National Endowment of the Arts Fellowship. She directs the creative writing program at Oklahoma State University and serves as poetry editor of the *Cimarron Review.*

Lyn Lifshin has over 120 books and has edited four anthologies. Recent books include *The Licorice Daughter: My Year with Ruffian* (Texas Review Press), *Another Woman Who Looks Like Me* (Black Sparrow at Godine). Forthcoming books include *Tsunami as History* (Poetryrepairs.com) and *A Girl Goes into the Woods* (New York Quarterly Books).

Frannie Lindsay's books are *Mayweed* (2009 Washington Prize, The Word Works), *Lamb* (Perugia, 2006), and *Where She Always Was* (Utah State University, 2004). "The Gathered Stones" will appear in *Our Vanishing* (Red Hen Press, 2014), winner of the 2012 Benjamin Saltman Award. She is the 2008 winner of the Missouri Review Prize. She has held fellowships from the National Endowment for the Arts and the Massachusetts Cultural Council. She is a classical pianist and lives in Belmont.

Ellaraine Lockie is a widely published and awarded poet, nonfiction book author and essayist. Her seventh chapbook, *Stroking David's Leg,* was awarded Best Individual Collection for 2010 from *Purple Patch* magazine in England, and her eighth chapbook, *Red for the Funeral,* won the 2010 San Gabriel Poetry Festival Chapbook Contest. Her chapbook, *Wild as in Familiar,* was a finalist in Finishing Line Press 2011 contest and has recently been released there. Ellaraine teaches poetry workshops and serves as Poetry Editor for the lifestyles magazine, *Lilipoh.*

Christina Lovin is the author of *What We Burned for Warmth* and *Little Fires.* A two-time Pushcart nominee and multi-award winner, her writing has appeared in numerous journals and anthologies. Southern Women Writers named Lovin 2007 Emerging Poet. Having served as Writer-in-Residence at Devil's Tower National Monument and the H.J. Andrews Experimental Forest in Central Oregon, in 2010, she served as inaugural Writer-in-Residence at Connemara, the NC home of the late poet Carl Sandburg. She resides with four dogs in a rural central Kentucky, where she is currently a lecturer at Eastern Kentucky University.

Alison Luterman is the author of *See How We Almost Fly* (Pearl Editions, 2010) and *The Largest Possible Life* (Pearl Editions, 2001). Her poems have appeared in *The Sun, Rattle, The Brooklyn Review, Oberon, Tattoo Highway, Kalliope, Poetry East, Poet Lore,* and elsehwere.

Marie-Elizabeth Mali is the author of *Steady, My Gaze* (Tebot Bach, 2011) and co-editor, with Annie Finch, of the anthology, *Villanelles* (Everyman's Library Pocket Poets, 2012). www.memali.com

"The layered inversion of meaning" describes one of Linda McCarriston's "chief poetic gifts" according to an astute *Kirkus* reviewer of her third book, *Little River*. McCarriston's second book, *Eva-Mary* (short-listed for the National Book Award), employs rhetorical and poetic strategies of the bardic tradition that animates narrative by involving spectator. She is from Lynn Mass, lives now in Gloucester, and teaches in the low residency MFA of the University of Alaska. *Talking Soft Dutch*, an AWP Selection, (Texas Tech) is her first book. She's written as well on poetry, class, and class-consciousness.

Deborah McGinn is an International Baccalaureate trained English and writing teacher at Lincoln High School and educated at the University of Nebraska at Lincoln. She earned a BA in English/Reading in Secondary Education, and an MA in English with a Creative Writing thesis. She has published in *The Iowa Review, South Dakota Review, English Journal, Plains Song Review, Plainsong, Times of Sorrow/Times of Grace, Untidy Season, Wild Goose Poetry Review, Platte Valley Review,* and *ARS Medica, a journal of medicine.*

Dawn McGuire is a neurologist and award-winning author of three poetry collections, including *Hands On* (ZYZZYVA, 2002) and *The Aphasia Café* (IFSF Publishing, 2012). She grew up in Eastern Kentucky and was educated at Princeton University, Union Theological Seminary, and the Columbia College of Physicians and Surgeons. She is the 2011 winner of the Sarah Lawrence/Campbell Corner Language Exchange Poetry Prize, awarded for "poems that treat larger themes with lyric intensity." McGuire is Professor of Neurology at Morehouse School of Medicine, and divides her time between Atlanta and the San Francisco Bay area.

Leslie Adrienne Miller's poetry collections include *Y* (Graywolf Press, 2012), *The Resurrection Trade, Eat Quite Everything You See, Yesterday Had a Man In It, Ungodliness* and *Staying Up For Love.* Recipient of a Loft McKnight Award of Distinction, two Minnesota State Arts Board Fellowships, a National Endowment for the Arts Fellowship in Poetry, as well as travel grants in Switzerland, Spain, Germany Scotland, France and Indonesia, she is Professor of English at the University of St. Thomas in St. Paul, Minnesota.

Tyler Mills is the author of *Tongue Lyre*, which won the 2011 Crab Orchard Series in Poetry First Book Award (Southern Illinois University Press). Her poems have appeared in *Antioch Review, Indiana Review, Georgia Review, Nashville Review, TriQuarterly Online,* and elsewhere; her poems have also been the recipient of awards from the *Crab Orchard Review, Gulf Coast,* and *Third Coast.* She lives in Chicago.

Deborah A. Miranda is the author of the collections, *Indian Cartography* (Greenfield Review Press, 1999), and *The Zen of La Llorona* (Salt Publishing, 2005), Miranda is an enrolled member of the Ohlone-Costanoan Esselen Nation of California, and is of Chumash and Jewish ancestry as well. Her mixed-genre manuscript *Bad Indians: A Tribal Memoir,* will be published by HeyDay Press in 2013, and her collection of essays, *The Hidden Stories of Isabel Meadows and Other California Indian Lacunae* is under contract with University of Nebraska Press. She is an Associate Professor of English at Washington and Lee University.

Lauren Moseley received her MFA from the University of North Carolina at Greensboro. She is a recipient of an artist's grant from the Money for Women/Barbara Deming Memorial Fund, and her poems have appeared or are forthcoming in *Arts & Letters, Best New Poets 2009, Cimarron Review, Lumina, West Branch Wired,* and elsewhere. Her poetry reviews can be found in *The Los Angeles Review, Pleiades,* and *storySouth.* She works at Algonquin Books in Chapel Hill, NC.

Sara-Luise Newman is a writer and artist in Oakland, CA. She holds California teaching credentials in Education and Art from Mills College and Sonoma State University, and has taught in various educational settings. She has studied with poets, Sharon Coleman at Berkeley City College, Susan Bono, and Patti Trimble, to name a few. She is published in *Milvia Street.* For the past seven years, Sara has run her preschool, Cottage in the Woods, out of her home. When she's not tending to the children and a menagerie of school pets, she manages to steal away to write.

Deena November graduated SUNY Binghamton in 2005 with a BA in Creative Writing, Poetry and received her MFA in Creative Writing, Poetry from Carlow University. In 2005, she co-edited the anthology *I Just Hope It's Lethal: Poems of Sadness, Madness, and Joy* (Houghton Mifflin). Her poems have also appeared in *Pittsburgh City Paper, Pittsburgh Post Gazette, Shaking Like a Mountain, Chiron Review, Voices in the Attic,* and *Keyhole Magazine.* She teaches at Carlow University and Robert Morris University. She co-created "Girls with Glasses" Reading Series, Workshops, and Literary Journal. Deena lives in Pittsburgh with her husband, daughter and dog.

Claire Ortalda, winner of the Georgia State University Fiction Prize and *Hackney and Fugue Magazine* awards, has been published in numerous literary journals, most recently *The Rattling Wall,* and *Eleven Eleven.* Her poem, "Iowa," was nominated for a Pushcart Prize. A former journalist, she is the editor of *The Other Side of the Closet* (IBS Press) and *Financial Sanity* (Doubleday).

Alicia Ostriker is author of twelve volumes of poetry, most recently *The Book of Seventy* (2009). She is also the author of *Writing Like a Woman and Stealing the Language: The Emergence of Women's Poetry in America, Feminist Revision and the Bible,* and *Dancing at the Devil's Party: Essays on Poetry, Politics and the Erotic.* Her poems have appeared in *The New Yorker, The Paris Review, The Nation, Poetry, American Poetry Review, The Atlantic,* and *MS.* She has received awards from the National Endowment for the Arts, the Poetry Society of America, the Rockefeller Foundation, and the Guggenheim Foundation.

Jennifer Perrine's collection of poems, *The Body Is No Machine* (New Issues, 2007), won the 2008 Devil's Kitchen Reading Award in Poetry. Her second book, *In the Human Zoo* (University of Utah Press, 2011), received the 2010 Agha Shahid Ali Poetry Prize. She currently teaches creative writing and gender studies at Drake University in Des Moines, Iowa.

Cati Porter is the author of *Seven Floors Up* (Mayapple Press), and the chapbooks *small fruit songs* (Pudding House), *(al)most delicious* (Dancing Girl Press), and *what Desire makes of us,* an e-chapbook with illustrations by Amy Payne (Ahadada Books). She edits the online journals *Poemeleon and Inlandia: A Literary Journey.*

Laura Van Prooyen is the author of *Inkblot and Altar* (Pecan Grove Press 2006). Her second collection of poems, *Resist,* was named a finalist for the 2011 Lexi Rudnitsky/Editor's Choice Award (Persea Books). Recent work is forthcoming in *The American Poetry Review, Boston Review,* and *Best of 32 Poems.* A recipient of grants from the American Association of University Women and the Barbara Deming Memorial Fund, she also has been awarded a Dorothy Sargent Rosenberg prize for her creative work. Van Prooyen earned an M.F.A. in Poetry at Warren Wilson College, and she lives in San Antonio, TX.

Natanya Ann Pulley's maternal family home is near Tuba City, AZ. She is half-Diné of the Kinyaa'áanii (Towering House Clan). Bicheii is Táchii'nii (Red Running Into Water Clan). Natanya is currently working on her Ph.D. at the University of Utah in Fiction Writing. She is an editor of *Quarterly West* and her work can be found in *Western Humanities Review, The Florida Review, Moon Milk Review, The Collagist* and on her site: gappsbasement.com. In addition to reading and studying experimental forms, disability and horror theory, Natanya enjoys being part of an unruly pack composed of her husband JP, their three psychic dogs, and a tank of fish.

Khadijah Queen is the author of two poetry collections, *Conduit* (Black Goat/Akashic, 2008), and *Black Peculiar,* which won the 2010 Noemi Press Book Award for Poetry. Individual poems appear in *jubilat, Best American Nonrequired Reading* (Houghton Mifflin, 2010) and *Villanelles* (Random House, 2012) and many other journals and anthologies. The recipient of fellowships from Cave Canem and the Norman Mailer Writers' Colony, she holds an MFA in creative writing from Antioch University Los Angeles.

Carol Quinn received a Ph.D. from the Creative Writing Program at the University of Houston in 2005, where she was the recipient of C. Glenn Cambor and Donald Barthelme Fellowships in Creative Writing. Currently, she is a visiting assistant professor teaching both creative writing and folkloristics at Towson University in Maryland. Her poetry has appeared in *Western Humanities Review, The Cincinnati Review, Pleiades, River Styx, The American Literary Review, The National Poetry Review, Alaska Quarterly Review,* and other journals.

Hilda Raz is the author of thirteen books including *What Happens* (University of Nebraska Press, 2009) and *All Odd and Splendid* (Wesleyan University Press, 2008). She serves as the Series Editor for Poetry at the University of New Mexico Press.

Tania Rochelle holds an MFA from The Program for Writers at Warren Wilson College. She has two books of poetry, *Karaoke Funeral* and *The World's Last Bone,* both published by Snake Nation Press. She has taught creative writing at Portfolio Center, in Atlanta, GA, for the past fourteen years and recently completed her Masters in Clinical Mental Health Counseling.

Dr. Kimberly Roppolo, of Cherokee, Choctaw, and Creek descent, is an Assistant Professor of English at the University of Oklahoma and affiliated faculty with the Native Studies program. She has published poems in journals and anthologies such as *Yellow Medicine Review, Red Ink, Studies in American Indian Literatures, Frontiers: A Journal of Women's Studies, CCTE Studies; Birthed from Scorched Hearts: Women Respond to War, Children of the Dragonfly, Simon J. Ortiz: A Poetic Legacy of Indigenous Continuance, Belonging, Commitment, This Bridge We Call Home: Radical Visions for Transformation,* and *The People Who Stayed: Southeastern Indian Writing After Removal.*

Lucinda Roy's publications include the poetry collections *Wailing the Dead to Sleep* and *The Humming Birds;* the novels *Lady Moses* and *The Hotel Alleluia;* and *No Right to Remain Silent: What We've Learned from the Tragedy at Virginia Tech,* a memoir-critique. She is an Alumni Distinguished Professor in English at Virginia Tech, where she teaches fiction, creative nonfiction, and poetry.

Carly Sachs is the recipient of the 2011 Stella Kupferberg Memorial Short Story Prize. Her first book of poems, *the steam sequence* won the 2006 Washington Writers' Publishing House book prize. She is the editor of *the why and later,* an anthology of poems that women have written about rape and sexual assault (deep cleveland press, 2007). Her poems have appeared in *The Best American Poetry 2004, Another Chicago Magazine, Nextbook, MiPoesis, PMS, The New Vilna Review, The Saint Ann's Review,* and *Present Tense.*

Elayne Safir is a fine artist and photographer, searching for glimpses of prehistoric magic and ancestral power among contemporary spaces and their inhabitants. She is deeply inspired by global citizenry, online tribal trends, the human noumena, the rich pantheistic folklore of Ukraine (her birthplace), and mythologies world-round. Her art has appeared on book covers, music albums, film sets, tattoos, and in gallery shows in Canada and the United States. She currently lives and works in New York City.

Marjorie Saiser's most recent book is *Beside You at the Stoplight* (Backwaters Press, 2010), winner of the Little Bluestem Award. Her work has been published or is forthcoming in *Prairie Schooner, Field, burntdistrict, Cimarron Review, Chatahoochee Review, Platte Valley Review,* and *Dos Passos Review.*

Ellin Sarot lives in Cambridge, Massachusetts. Her poems have appeared in *Chamindade Literary Review, Women's Studies, The Beloit Poetry Journal,* and *The Little Review,* among other periodicals, and her reviews have appeared in *The Women's Review of Books.*

Jane Satterfield is the author of *Daughters of Empire: A Memoir of a Year in Britain and Beyond* (Demeter, 2009) and two poetry collections: *Assignation at Vanishing Point* (Elixir Press Book Award) and *Shepherdess with an Automatic* (Washington Writers' Publishing House, Towson

University Prize). Among her awards are an NEA Fellowship in poetry and the Faulkner Society Gold Medal in the Essay, as well as residencies in poetry or nonfiction from the Virginia Center for the Creative Arts.

Maureen Seaton's recent publications include her sixth solo poetry collection *Cave of the Yellow Volkswagen* (Carnegie Mellon University Press, 2009), a poetry chapbook *America Loves Carney* (Sow's Ear, 2009), and a memoir *Sex Talks to Girls* (University of Wisconsin Press, 2008), winner of the Lambda Literary Award. She co-edited, with Denise Duhamel and David Trinidad, the anthology *Saints of Hysteria: A Half-Century of Collaborative American Poetry* (Soft Skull Press, 2006). The recipient of an NEA Fellowship in poetry and two Pushcart Prizes for individual poems, Seaton teaches poetry, literary collage, and collaboration at the University of Miami, Coral Gables, Florida.

Danielle Sellers is originally from Key West, FL. She has an MA from The Writing Seminars at Johns Hopkins University and an MFA from the University of Mississippi where she held the Grisham Poetry Fellowship. Her poems have appeared or are forthcoming in *Subtropics, Smartish Pace, Cimarron Review, Poet Lore, Prairie Schooner, 32 Poems,* and elsewhere. Her book, *Bone Key Elegies*, was published in 2009 by Main Street Rag. Last summer, she was awarded a Walter E. Dakin Poetry fellowship to attend the Sewanee Writers' Conference. She's editor of *The Country Dog Review* and teaches at the University of Mississippi.

BT Shaw lives, works, and eats pie in Portland, Oregon. She teaches at Portland State University and the Independent Publishing Resource Center, and she's edited *The Oregonian's* poetry column for fifteen years. Her work has appeared in a variety of journals, including *Field, Orion,* and *AGNI*, and her collection, *This Dirty Little Heart*, won the 2007 Blue Lynx Prize.

Larissa Shmailo's work has appeared in *Gargoyle, Brooklyn Rail, American Translator, Newsweek, Barrow Street, Drunken Boat, Fulcrum, The Unbearables Big Book of Sex,* and over thirty anthologies. Her books of poetry are *In Paran* (BlazeVOX), the chapbook *A Cure for Suicide* (Cervena Barva Press), and the e-book *Fib Sequence* (Argotist Ebooks); her poetry CDs are *The No-Net World* and *Exorcism*, available through iTunes and other digital distributors. Her original translation of Alexei Kruchenych's libretto, *Victory over the Sun,* is forthcoming from Cervena Barva Press. larissashmailo.blogspot.com

Evie Shockley is the author of four poetry collections, including *the new black* (Wesleyan, 2011), *a half-red sea* (Carolina Wren Press, 2006), and two chapbooks; she has also published a book of criticism, *Renegade Poetics: Black Aesthetics and Formal Innovation in African American Poetry* (Iowa, 2011). Her poetry has been recognized with a *Library Journal* citation for Best Books of 2011, a nomination for a 2012 Hurston/Wright Legacy Award, and the 2012 Holmes National Poetry Prize. She teaches African American literature and creative writing at Rutgers University-New Brunswick.

Cassie Premo Steele Ph.D., is the author of nine books about the healing power of words and creativity in women's lives—three books of poetry, an audio poetry album, a novel, and four books of non-fiction, including *We Heal from Memory*, about the ways multicultural American women's poetry helps us witness to traumatic histories. Her poetry has been nominated twice for the Pushcart Prize. cassiepremosteele.com

Margo Taft Stever's chapbook, *The Hudson Line* (Main Street Rag, 2012) was an editor's choice. Her first full-length collection, *Frozen Spring* (2002), was the winner of the Mid-List Press First Series Award for Poetry. Her chapbook, *Reading the Night Sky*, won the 1996 Riverstone Poetry Chapbook Competition. Her poems, essays, and reviews have appeared in magazines and anthologies including *The Webster Review, Ironwood, New England Review, Minnesota Review, West Branch, Seattle Review,* and *No More Masks* (first edition). She is the founder of The Hudson Valley Writers' Center and the founding editor of Slapering Hol Press.

Alison Stone's poems have appeared in *The Paris Review, Poetry, Ploughshares, Barrow Street, Poet Lore,* and a variety of other journals and anthologies. She has been awarded Poetry's Frederick Bock Prize and *New York Quarterly's* Madeline Sadin award. Her first book, *They Sing at Midnight,* won the 2003 Many Mountains Moving Poetry Award and was published by Many Mountains Moving Press. *From the Fool to the World,* a chapbook of poems, is forthcoming from Parallel Press. With the poet Kathi Aguero she is currently editing an anthology of poems on the Persephone/Demeter myth.

Billie R. Tadros is a doctoral student in English Literature at the University of Louisiana at Lafayette and a graduate of the MFA program in Poetry at Sarah Lawrence College. Her poem "Reactor" was recently chosen by Sandra Beasley for the 2012 Yellowwood Prize in Poetry. Her work has recently appeared in *Barely South Review* and *Yalobusha Review.*

Kathleen Tyler lives in Los Angeles where she teaches English at a local high school. Her publications include *The Secret Box* (Mayapple Press) and *My Florida* (Backwaters Press). Her poems have appeared in numerous journals including *The Rattling Wall* (Pen/USA), *Visions International, Runes, Solo, Poetry Motel, Margie, Seems, Cider Press Review,* and others. She has been the featured reader at many Southern California venues. A poem from *My Florida* was nominated for a Pushcart Prize.

Judith Vollmer's books of poetry include *The Water Books* (Autumn House), *Reactor,* (University of Wisconsin Press), *The Door Open to the Fire* (Cleveland State University Press), *Level Green* (Wisconsin), and *Black Butterfly* (Center for Book Arts, limited edition). Vollmer is the recipient of poetry fellowships from the National Endowment for the Arts and the Pennsylvania Council on the Arts. She co-edits the international poetry journal *5 AM* and lives in Pittsburgh. www.judithvollmer.com

Megan Welch has been a gluttonous creative since birth, spinning her way through more than 35 job titles in theater, film, art, and business including costume designer, clown, bookkeeper and (of course!) waitress. Recently retired from bookkeeping, she has turned to writing to fill her days and her heart. She has published four chapbooks for friends and family.

Tana Jean Welch currently lives in Tallahassee where she is completing a Ph.D. in Literature at Florida State University. Her poems have appeared in *Beloit Poetry Journal, The Southern Review, The Gettysburg Review, Prairie Schooner,* and other national literary journals.

Judy Wells received her B.A. from Stanford and her Ph.D. in Comparative Literature from UC Berkeley. She taught writing in Bay Area colleges before a career as an Academic Counselor at St. Mary's College of California and as a faculty member of St. Mary's Graduate Liberal Studies Program. She has published nine collections of poetry: *I Dream of Circus Characters: A Berkeley Chronicle* (2010), *Little Lulu Talks with Vincent Van Gogh* (2007), *Call Home* (2005), *Everything Irish* (1999), *The Calling: Twentieth Century Women Artists* (1994), *The Part-time Teacher* (1991), *Jane, Jane* (1981), *Albuquerque Winter* (1980), and *I Have Berkeley* (1979).

Monica Wendel is the author of *No Apocalypse* (forthcoming, Georgetown Review Press) and the chapbook *Call it a Window* (Midwest Writing Center, 2012). She holds a BA in philosophy from the State University of New York at Geneseo and an MFA in poetry writing from New York University. A recipient of NYU's Goldwater and Starworks teaching fellowships, she has taught writing at Goldwater Hospital, St. Mary's Health Care Center for Kids, NYU, and St. Thomas Aquinas College. In 2013, she will serve as the writer-in-residence at the Kerouac Project of Orlando, Florida.

Amber West is a poet, playwright, and educator. Her writing has appeared in journals such as *Calyx* and *Journal of Research on Women & Gender,* and in the edited volume, *Episodes from a History of Undoing: The Heritage of Female Subversiveness* (Cambridge Scholars, 2012). She earned her MFA in Poetry at NYU, and is a doctoral candidate at University of Connecticut where her research focuses on contemporary feminist poetry, puppetry and hybrid performance. Her plays and "puppet poems" have been performed in theaters in SF and NYC. She lives in Brooklyn where she's co-founder the artist collective, Alphabet Arts www.alphabetarts.org.

July Westhale is a fierce femme writer with a weakness for botany and hot air balloons. She has been awarded fellowships from Lambda, *Tin House,* and the Dairy Hollow Writers Colony. Some of her recent work can be found at *WordRiot, 580 Split, Quarterly West, Muzzle, Roar,* and *So to Speak: A Feminist Literary Journal.* She was recently nominated for the Best New Poets of 2012. www.julywesthale.com

Rosemary Winslow lives in downtown Washington, D.C., and teaches at The Catholic University of America. Her book *Green Bodies* expressed and grappled with the complexities of love in troubled families, and sought understanding, forgiveness, and compassion for the wide circle of humankind. She has taught in shelters for women, and now enjoys yoga, hiking, swimming, kayaking, and singing in a choir. At present she is writing about caring and working with the very ill and dying at a hospital.

Karenne Wood is an enrolled member of the Monacan Indian Nation. A Ph.D. candidate and Ford Fellow in anthropology at the University of Virginia, she works to revitalize indigenous languages and cultural practices. Wood's first book, *Markings on Earth,* won the North American Native Authors Award for Poetry in 2000. She edited *The Virginia Indian Heritage Trail,* now in its third edition, and she recently wrote a chapter on Southeastern Indians for National Geographic's *Indian Nations of North America.* In 2009 she spoke at a United Nations' Permanent Forum on Indigenous Issues event on "The Politics of Writing."

Susan Yount was born and raised on a 164 acre farm in southern Indiana where she learned to drive a tractor and hug her beloved goat, Cinnamon. She is editor and publisher of the *Arsenic Lobster Poetry Journal* and madam of the Chicago Poetry Bordello. She founded Misty Publications. She works full-time at the Associated Press and teaches online poetry classes at The Rooster Moans Poetry Cooperative. Her chapbook, *Catastrophe Theory,* is just out from Hyacinth Girl Press.

Andrena Zawinski's poetry collection, *Something About* from Blue Light Press in San Francisco, is a 2010 PEN Oakland Josephine Miles Award recipient. Her first collection, *Traveling in Reflected Light,* from Pig Iron Press in Youngstown, Ohio is a Kenneth Patchen Prize in Poetry. She runs a Women's Poetry Salon in the San Francisco Bay Area for which she is editor of their collection, *Turning a Train of Thought Upside Down: An Anthology of Women's Poetry.* She is also Features Editor for *PoetryMagazine.com* and a teacher of creative writing.

ABOUT THE EDITOR

Laura Madeline Wiseman has a doctorate from the University of Nebraska-Lincoln where she teaches English and creative writing. She is the author of seven collections of poetry, including the full-length book, *Sprung* (San Francisco Bay Press, 2012), the letterpress books *Unclose the Door* (Gold Quoin Press, 2012) and *Farm Hands* (Gold Quoin Press, 2012), and the chapbooks *She Who Loves Her Father* (Dancing Girl Press, 2012), *Branding Girls* (Finishing Line Press, 2011), *Ghost Girl* (Pudding House Publications, 2010), and *My Imaginary* (Dancing Girl Press, 2010). Her work has appeared in *Prairie Schooner, Margie, Arts & Letters, Poet Lore,* and *Feminist Studies.* She has received an Academy of American Poets Award, a Mari Sandoz/Prairie Schooner Award, a Susan Atefact Peckham Fellowship, a Center for the Great Plains Studies grant, and a Wurlitzer Foundation fellowship. www.lauramadelinewiseman.com

Works Cited for the Critical Introduction

Berns, Nancy. "Degendering the Problem and Gendering the Blame: Political Discourse on Women's Violence." *Gender & Society*, Vol. 15 No. 2, April 2001, 262-281.

Brown, Deborah, Annie Finch and Maxine Kumin, Eds. *Lofty Dogmas: Poets on Poetics.* Fayetteville: University of Arkansas Press, 2005.

Crenshaw, Kimberle Williams. "Mapping the Margins: Intersectionality, Identity Politics, and Violence Against Women of Color." *The Public Nature of Private Violence.* Martha Albertson Finneman and Roxanne Mykitiuk, Eds. New York: Routledge, 1994. 93-118.

Chrystos. "Accident." *Not Vanishing.* Vancouver: Press Gang Publishers, 1988.

DeShazer, Mary K. *A Poetics of Resistance: Women Writing in El Salvador, South Africa, and the United States.* Ann Arbor: University of Michigan Press, 1994.

Flannery, Kathryn. "The Passion of Conviction: Reclaiming Polemic for a Reading of Second-Wave Feminism." *Rhetoric Review.* 20.5 (2001) 113-129.

Forché, Carolyn, Ed. "Introduction." *Against Forgetting: Twentieth Century Poetry of Witness.* New York: Norton, 1993.

Glenn, Cheryl. "Silence: A Rhetorical Art for Resisting Disciplines(s)," *JAC 22.2* (Spring 2002).

Graham, Jorie. "From Introduction to The Best American Poetry 1990." *Lofty Dogmas: Poets on Poetics.* Brown, Deborah, Annie Finch and Maxine Kumin, eds. Fayetteville: University of Arkansas Press, 2005.

Grahn, Judy. Work of a Common Woman: The Collected Poetry of Judy Grahn: 1964-1977. New York: St. Martin's Press, 1978.

Lorde, Audre. "Poetry is Not a Luxury." *Lofty Dogmas: Poets on Poetics.* Brown, Deborah, Annie Finch and Maxine Kumin, eds. Fayetteville: University of Arkansas Press, 2005.

Lorde, Audre. "The Transformation of Silence into Language and Action." *Sister Outsider.* Berkeley: Cross Press, 1984.

Martin, Biddy and Chandra Talpade Mohanty. "Feminist Politics: What's Home Got to Do with It?" *Feminisms: An Anthology of Literary Theory and Criticism.* Robyn R. Worhol and Diane Price Herndl, eds. New Brunswick: Rutgers University Press, 1997.

Milosz, Czeslaw. "Nobel Prize Lecture, 1980." *Lofty Dogmas: Poets on Poetics.* Brown, Deborah, Annie Finch and Maxine Kumin, eds. Fayetteville: University of Arkansas Press, 2005.

Minh-ha, Trinh T. *Woman Native Other: Writing Postcoloniality and Feminism.* Bloomington: Indiana University Press, 1989.

Neruda, Pablo. "From Toward the Splendid City, Nobel Lecture, 1971." *Lofty Dogmas: Poets on Poetics.* Brown, Deborah, Annie Finch and Maxine Kumin, eds. Fayetteville: University of Arkansas Press, 2005.

Oles, Carole and Hilda Raz. "The Feminist Literary Movement." *Poetry After Modernism.* Robert McDowell, Ed. Revised Expanded Edition. New York: Story Line Press, 1998.

Ostriker, Alicia Suskin. *Stealing the Language.* Boston: Beacon Press, 1986.

Pratt, Minne Bruce. *Crime Against Nature.* New York: Firebrand Press, 1990.

Rich, Adrienne. *What is Found There: Notebooks on Poetry and Poetics.* Exp. Edition. New York: W.W. Norton & Company, Inc. 2003.

Russo, Mary. "Female Grotesques: Carnival and Theory." *Feminist Studies: Critical Studies.* Teresa De Lauretis, ed. Bloomington: Indiana University Press, 1985.

Sandoval, Chela. *Methodology of the Oppressed.* Minneapolis: University of Minnesota, 2000.

Sandoval, Chela. "U.S. Third World Feminism: The Theory and Method of Oppositional Consciousness in the Postmodern World." *Genders* 10 (spring 1991): 14.

Scarry, Elaine. *The Body in Pain: The Making and Unmaking of the World.* Oxford: Oxford University Press, 1987

Schoerke, Meg. "The Armor of Outside." *Poetry After Modernism.* Revised Expanded Edition. Robert McDowell, Ed. New York: Story Line Press, 1998.

Shelley, Percy Bysshe. "From A Defense of Poetry." *Lofty Dogmas: Poets on Poetics.* Brown, Deborah, Annie Finch and Maxine Kumin, eds. Fayetteville: University of Arkansas Press, 2005.

Spry, Tami. "In the Absence of Word and Body: Hegemonic Implications of 'Victim' and 'Survivor' in Women's Narratives of Sexual Violence." *Women and Language* 18.2 (Fall 1995): 27-32.

Wittig, Monique. *The Straight Mind and Other Essays.* Boston: Beacon Press, 1992.

----

[1] Rich, Adrienne. "Ghazals: Homage to Ghalib." *The Fact of a Doorframe: Poems Selected and New 1950-2001,* New York: Norton, 2002. 107.

[2] I take up Henry Wallace's definition of family violence which defines violence as "any act or omission by persons who are cohabitating that results in serious injury to other members of the family" (2). This anthology's definition extends Wallace's definition to point to the significance of gender in issues of violence against women. Wallace, Harvey, Ed. *Family Violence: Legal, Medical, and Social Perspectives.* Fourth Edition. Boston: Pearson, 2005. For extended definitions on family violence, gender violence, and other forms of intimate violence see Wallace.

[3] Emerson, Ralph Waldo. "From The Poet." *Lofty Dogmas: Poets on Poetics.* Brown, Deborah, Annie Finch and Maxine Kumin, eds. Fayetteville: University of Arkansas Press, 2005. 36.

[4] Rich, Adrienne. "As if your life depended on it." *What is Found There: Notebooks on Poetry and Poetics.* New York: Norton, 2003.

[5] Sandoval, Chela. "U.S. Third World Feminism: The Theory and Method of Oppositional Consciousness in the Postmodern World." *Genders* 10 (spring 1991): 14.

[6] Sandoval, 3.

[7] Pope, Alexander. "An Essay on Criticism." *Lofty Dogmas: Poets on Poetics.* Deborah Brown, Annie Finch and Maxine Kumin, eds. Fayetteville: University of Arkansas Press, 2005. 146.

[8] Harjo, Joy and Gloria Bird, eds. *Reinventing the Enemy's Language: Contemporary Native Women's Writing of North America.* New York: Simon, 1996.

Made in the USA
San Bernardino, CA
01 March 2015